MEANING

BY

Stephen R. Schiffer

OXFORD

AT THE CLARENDON PRESS

1972

Oxford University Press, Ely House, London W. 1

GLASGOW NEW YORK TORONTO MELBOURNE WELLINGTON
CAPE TOWN IBADAN NAIROBI DAR ES SALAAM LUSAKA ADDIS ABABA
DELHI BOMBAY CALCUTTA MADRAS KARACHI LAHORE DACCA
KUALA LUMPUR SINGAPORE HONG KONG TOKYO

PRINTED IN GREAT BRITAIN
AT THE UNIVERSITY PRESS, OXFORD
BY VIVIAN RIDLER
PRINTER TO THE UNIVERSITY

For

Samuel G. Schiffer

ACKNOWLEDGEMENTS

I have benefited from discussion with many people, but my conversations with Gareth Evans, R. M. Harnish, David Lewis, M. C. Mosher, and George Myro were especially helpful. I could not be much more indebted than I am to H. P. Grice, B. F. Loar, and P. F. Strawson. Were it not for my conversations with them this work would be considerably worse than it is.

I thank the secretaries of the philosophy department at the University of California, Berkeley, and especially Jane Babcock, for expert typing.

CONTENTS

V. UTTERANCE-MEANING AND CONVENTION

VI. UTTERANCE-MEANING AND LANGUAGE

I

INTRODUCTION TO A THEORY
OF MEANING

I.1 *Some meanings of 'Meaning'*

W H A T is meaning? That is the question I shall be primarily concerned to answer in this essay—at least for those senses of 'meaning' and its cognates especially relevant to an understanding of language and communication.

That is our question, but we will not get very far by asking it. We might instead try asking, what is it for something x to mean something? An answer to this question, it would seem, would put us some way toward an understanding of the concept of meaning. The trouble with this question is that utterances of the form 'x means something' may be true in at least two different ways. For consider the following two sentences.

(1) Seymour meant something.
(2) That mark means something.

If (1) is true, then it is most likely that Seymour *did* something. But if (2) is true, it is unlikely that that mark did something. If (2) is true, then it will be true that that mark has meaning. But if Seymour means something it is unlikely that he has meaning. (Unlikely but not impossible. Seymour may mean something in the same way that, say, a signal flag means something. Thus, a lighthouse keeper might communicate to ships at sea that there is a hurricane coming by putting his son Seymour on the top of the lighthouse, in which case any sailor worth his salt would know that Seymour meant "there is a hurricane coming".)

For the moment, let us write 'means$_s$' for the sense (or senses) of 'means' appropriate to sentences like (1) and 'means$_x$' for the sense (or senses) of 'means' appropriate to sentences like (2). Then the question "What is meaning?" is seen to include the following two questions.

(1) What is it for someone S to mean$_s$ something?
(2) What is it for something x to mean$_x$ something?

Questions (1) and (2) divide into still further questions.

There are two senses in which a person can usually be said to mean or have meant something. If S meant$_s$ something, then it may be that there was something x such that

> (1a) S meant that . . . by (or in) producing (or doing) x.

For example:

> By (or in) uttering 'The cat is on the mat', S meant that the cat was on the mat.
>
> By (or in) waving his handkerchief S meant that the coast was clear.
>
> By (or in) uttering 'Shut the door!' S meant that you were to shut the door.

If S meant$_s$ something, then it may also be that there was something x such that

> (1b) S meant ". . ." by x.[1]

For example:

> When he said 'My uncle owns a cape' S meant "promontory of land" by 'cape'.
>
> S meant "his male parent is inexperienced" by 'his father is green'.

Utterances of form (1a) are used to report the "message" S was communicating; that is, quite roughly, the "information" S was communicating or the "directive" S was issuing. Thus, if S meant that . . . by uttering x, then the only proper substituends for '. . .' will be sentences—expressions which express a complete thought or action, as they say in the grammar books. Utterances

---

[1] Something ought to be said about my use of quotation marks. Single quotes (' ') are generally used only when I am talking about the expression contained therein, but occasionally a variable is used both without and within single quotes where it is clear from the context that whatever is a substituend for the one occurrence is a substituend for the other occurrence (thus I might write: 'suppose someone says 'I tell you that p' intending his audience to think that p'). Double quotes (" ") are used in the following ways. (1) They are used for the citation of articles. (2) They are used as "scare quotes". (3) They are sometimes used to quote the (real or imagined) words of another. (4) They are always used in the specification of the meaning of an expression: e.g., 'bachelor' means "unmarried man". (5) Derivatively upon (4), they are used to specify the sense of an expression intended by a speaker: e.g., by 'cape' John meant "promontory of land". With respect to uses (4) and (5), nothing much is intended by this conventional device, except to indicate that the expression enclosed in double quotes is being used to specify the sense or intended sense of some other expression; when a variable occurs within double quotes we obtain a specification of meaning by replacing the variable with a substituend for the variable (cf. William P. Alston, *Philosophy of Language*, p. 21).

of form (1b), on the other hand, are used to report the sense or meaning of x S intended x to have (or to be operative) on the occasion of his producing (or doing) x. Thus, if S meant "...'" by x, then the proper substituend for '...' may be a word, a phrase, or a sentence.

It is possible for S to mean something by (or in) producing (or doing) x without meaning something by x, and it is possible for S to mean something by x without meaning something by (or in) producing (or doing) x. For example, S meant that he was bored by wiggling his ears (he was, say, communicating to his wife by this non-conventional means that he was bored); but in such a case it is unlikely that S meant something by his ear wiggle, since it is unlikely that S thought that an ear wiggle had meaning. And, for example, by 'he is blue', S may mean "he is sad" but not mean anything by uttering 'he is blue': 'he is blue' may have been part of the longer utterance 'he is blue or he is tired', or S may have uttered 'he is blue' in the course of reciting a poem.

In general, if S utters a sentence σ and means thereby that p, then it will also be the case that S meant "p" by σ. But this need not be so; for example, it might be that when S uttered 'I'm in hock' he meant "I'm in debt" by 'I'm in hock' (i.e. S intended the expression 'I'm in hock' to have the same sense as 'I'm in debt' and not, say, 'I'm in white Rhine wine'); but it may also be that S was speaking ironically and that by uttering 'I'm in hock' S meant that he was in excellent financial shape.

So the question "What is it for someone to mean$_s$ something?" divides into the two questions: "What is it for someone to mean something by (or in) producing (or doing) x?" and "What is it for someone to mean something by x?" And this gives us the following analysanda.

(1a) S meant something by (or in) producing (or doing) x. (S meant [that] ... by (or in) producing (or doing) x);

and

(1b) S meant something by x. (S meant "..." by x).

(The part in parentheses is to remind us that we do not want an account of what it is to mean something which does not enable us to specify what was meant.)

Question (2),"What is it for something x to mean$_x$ something?", also divides into further questions.

The class of things which both mean something and have meaning may be divided into four subclasses: (1) the class of whole-utterance types, such things as sentences and signals; (2) the class of whole-utterance tokens; (3) the class of part-utterance types, such things as words and phrases; and (4) the class of part-utterance tokens. For membership in these four classes we may give the following conditions of adequacy. (1) A type x is a whole-utterance type if and only if x means (timeless) ". . ." and the only proper substituends for '. . .' are complete sentences. (2) A token x is a whole-utterance token if and only if x is a token of a whole-utterance type. (3) A type x is a part-utterance type if and only if x means (timeless) ". . ." and the only proper substituends for '. . .' are words and/or phrases. (4) A token x is a part-utterance token if and only if x is a token of a part-utterance type.

We have, then, the following additional analysanda.

(2a$_1$) x is a whole-utterance type
(x is a whole-utterance type which means ". . .".)

(2a$_2$) x is a whole-utterance token
(x is a whole-utterance token which means ". . .".)

(2b$_1$) x is a part-utterance type
(x is a part-utterance type which means ". . .".)

(2b$_2$) x is a part-utterance token
(x is a part-utterance token which means ". . .".)

It may seem that even if we provide correct analyses for (1a)–(2b$_2$) we shall still not have a complete analysis of the relevant concept of meaning; for we should still have sentences of the following forms to worry about.

(3) The (a) meaning of x is ". . .".
e.g., The meaning of 'vixen' is "female fox".

(4) x has meaning.
e.g., 'Horse' has meaning.

(5) x is meaningful (less).
e.g., 'cat mat on is the' is meaningless.

(6) x has two meanings.
e.g., 'Cape' has two meanings.

(7) x means the same as y.
e.g., 'Vixen' means the same as 'female fox' .

(8) The meaning of x includes the meaning of y.
e.g., The meaning of 'bachelor' includes the meaning of 'unmarried'.

However, (3)–(5) reduce to (2a)–(2b₂). For: a meaning of x is
"..." if and only if x means "..."; x has meaning if and only if x
means something; x is meaningful if and only if x means something; and x is meaningless if and only if it is not the case that x
means something. And while (6)–(8) do not directly reduce to
(2a)–(2b₂), if correct analyses can be provided for (2a)–(2b₂), it
will then only be a short step to doing the same for (6)–(8) and
any similar concepts. I submit, then, that if correct analyses are
provided for (1a)–(2b₂) we shall have answered or virtually
answered the question "What is meaning?"—at least for those
senses of 'meaning' and its cognates especially and directly relevant to an understanding of language and communication.

Of course not every sense of 'meaning' and its cognates is
especially and directly relevant to an understanding of language
and communication, and there are senses which are so relevant
but which we should want to keep separate from the senses we
shall be concerned with.

(1) By uttering 'that ignoble cretin' he meant you.
(2) I meant what I said when I said that I hate you.
(3) Your love means more to me than all the tea in China.
(4) I meant that [e.g., my putting a mouse in your bed] as
    a joke.
(5) I meant to scare you by throwing the knife.
(6) Those footprints mean that someone was here.

(1)–(6) are roughly equivalent to (1′)–(6′) respectively.

(1′) By uttering 'that ignoble cretin' he was referring to you.
(2′) I was sincere and serious in saying that I hate you.
(3′) Your love is more important to me than all the tea in
    China.
(4′) I intended that as a joke.
(5′) I intended to scare you by throwing the knife.
(6′) Those footprints indicate (imply) that someone was
    here.

No doubt there are important connections between at least some
of these senses of 'mean' and the senses we shall be concerned
with (Grice's "natural"–"non-natural" classification is highly
suggestive in this respect). Nevertheless, these connections will
not be explored by me, and my sole purpose in listing these
examples is to put them out of the way.

I.2 *An order of priorities*

Let us say in an old-fashioned and unrefined way that a concept ϕ is "logically prior" to a concept ψ if (1) the concept ϕ enters into the analysis of ψ but (2) the concept ψ does not enter into the analysis of ϕ.

What can be said about the order of priorities obtaining between our four analysanda, (1a)–(2b)? (In this section I ignore (2a$_2$) and (2b$_2$).) It would be naïve to suppose that this question could be settled independently of a complete theory of meaning, but a preliminary and tentative attempt to answer this question may make clear some of the rationale behind starting out in one way rather than another.

First, is (2a), the concept of a whole-utterance type, logically prior to (2b), the concept of a part-utterance type, or vice versa, or neither? A prima facie reason for thinking that the concept of a whole-utterance type cannot be logically prior to the concept of a part-utterance type is that the meaning of a sentence is partly a function of the meaning of its words. On the other hand, there are stronger reasons for thinking that the notion of a whole-utterance type is logically prior to the notion of a part-utterance type. In the first place, not all whole-utterance types are like sentences in being composite or structured; some, such as an air-raid whistle, are *non-composite*. A whole-utterance type x, we may say, is non-composite just in case there is no "proper part" of x, y, such that both y means something and the meaning of x is determined in part by the meaning of y. So if, as it seems reasonable to suppose, a single and univocal account can be given of what it is for something to be a whole-utterance type, such an account will be independent of the notion of a part-utterance type. In the second place, something is a part-utterance type only if it is the sort of thing which when combined in certain ways with certain other things yields a whole-utterance type.

It is clear that (1b), the concept of someone meaning something by x, cannot be logically prior to (2a); for S can mean "…" by x only if (S believes that) x already means "…". However, this does not commit us to the view that either (2a) or (2b) is logically prior to (1b): perhaps (1b)–(2b) are each to be analysed in terms of an account of (1a), an account, that is, of what it is for someone to mean something by (or in) producing (or doing) x.

This leaves us with the crucial question: which is logically prior, (1a) or (2a)? There are two considerations which together give us good reason to suppose that (1a) is logically prior to (2a). In the first place, x is a whole-utterance type which means, say, "snow is white" only if people do, would, or could mean that snow is white by uttering x. Roughly speaking and with reservations, one knows what a whole-utterance type x means only if one knows what a person would normally or ordinarily mean by uttering x. In the second place, it is possible for a person to mean something by uttering x even though x has no meaning. For example, in suitable circumstances S might communicate to an audience A that he, S, is angry by uttering the sound 'grrr'. In such an event, S may intend A to recognize that 'grrr' resembles the sound dogs make when they are angry and to infer in part therefrom that S's intention in uttering 'grrr' was to inform A that S was angry.

Let us hereinafter refer to an account of what it is for someone S to mean something by (or in) producing (or doing) x as an account of S-meaning. Now the above considerations do not prove that an account of S-meaning can be given which is logically prior to accounts of (1b)–(2b), and certain general objections will shortly be considered to such a claim, but these considerations do give us reason for beginning our enterprise by seeking to provide an account of S-meaning, one which is not in terms of any semantic notions. Such an account has been offered by Professor H. P. Grice in his article, "Meaning". Not only is Grice's account highly illuminating, it is also, so far as I know, the only published attempt ever made by a philosopher or anyone else to say precisely and completely what it is for someone to mean something. We will do well to consider it in some detail.

I.3 Grice's account of S-meaning

Three preliminary remarks are in order before presenting Grice's account.

(1) Grice is concerned to analyse those senses of 'meaning' especially relevant to an understanding of language and communication, and he uses the label 'non-natural meaning' both to mark those senses and to distinguish them from those senses of 'meaning' and its cognates typified by expressions such as 'he meant to put salt in his soup' and 'those spots mean measles', which Grice labels 'natural meaning'. Since we shall only be

B

concerned with non-natural meaning, the qualification may be dropped.

(2) Grice uses 'utterance' and its cognates in an artificially extended way which includes non-linguistic items and behaviour. I will continue this artificial use, so that now an account of S-meaning becomes an account of what it is for a person S to mean something by (or in) uttering (an utterance) x.

(3) What Grice offers us is an account of what it is for someone to mean something by (an utterance) x. Grice did not distinguish between the two lately distinguished senses in which a person could be said to have meant something, but it is clear that if his analysans has any application at all, it is as an analysans for what it is for someone to mean something by (or in) uttering x. The needed correction will be made in the restatements below and in our discussion of Grice's account.

Grice presents his analysis informally and succinctly. He first suggests that

'[S] meant something by x' is (roughly) equivalent to '[S] intended the utterance of x to produce some effect in an audience by means of the recognition of this intention' ("Meaning", p. 385);

but this is soon qualified, so that:

the intended effect must be something which in some sense is within the control of the audience, or that in some sense of 'reason' the recognition of the intention behind x is for the audience a reason and not merely a cause.

This qualification is needed in order to rule out a possible counter-example.

Suppose I discovered some person so constituted that, when I told him that whenever I grunted in a special way I wanted him to blush or to incur some physical malady, thereafter whenever he recognized the grunt (and with it my intention), he did blush or incur the malady.

Should he then grunt, we should not, Grice thinks, want to say that he thereby meant something.

Let us look more closely at Grice's account, making some needed distinctions along the way.

1. According to Grice, S meant something by uttering x only if S intended his utterance of x to produce some effect in an

audience *A*. Taken widely or narrowly enough, this could be read in one or another of three different ways.

(1) There is an effect *e* such that *S* meant something by uttering *x* only if *S* intended his utterance of *x* to produce *e* in an audience *A*.

(2) *S* meant something by uttering *x* only if *S* intended that there be an effect *e* such that his utterance of *x* produce *e* in an audience *A*.

(3) *S* meant something by uttering *x* only if there is an effect *e* such that *S* intended his utterance of *x* to produce *e* in an audience *A*.

Clearly, (1) is not intended: we are not to think that there is a certain effect, say, believing that Caesar was a Turk, such that one means something by uttering something only if one intends someone to believe that Caesar was a Turk. Now in the case of (3) *S* must have in mind a particular effect which he intends to produce in *A*, whereas in the case of (2) *S* may merely intend that some effect, no matter what, gets produced in *A*. Since, amongst other things, Grice says that we know what was meant just in case we know what effect *S* intended to produce in *A* (by means of recognition of intention), it is fairly clear that he intended us to take his account of *S*-meaning as committing him to (3). In the restatement of Grice's account below, we shall express this informally by saying that *S* meant something by uttering *x* only if *S* uttered *x* intending to produce a *certain* response *r* in an audience *A*.

A similar problem arises with regard to the intended audience. And here, too, I think we are at least provisionally to understand Grice as meaning that *S* must intend to produce an effect in a *certain* audience *A*; that is, *S* means something by uttering *x* only if there is an audience *A* and a response *r* such that *S* intends his utterance of *x* to produce *r* in *A*. There are several reasons why this latest refinement should be taken as provisional. In the first place, even if *S* must intend to produce a response in a particular person, the "particular person" he has in mind may not exist. In the second place, it does not appear to be a necessary condition for *S* meaning something by uttering *x* that he intends to produce a response in a particular person. If *S* is drowning, he may shout 'Help!' intending anyone who hears him to come to his rescue. And in the third place, we are here quantifying into an intensional context and this may license inferences we might not otherwise be willing to tolerate. (Grice is also, of course, quantifying into an intensional context in the case of the intended response, but here the relevant effects, being actions and psychological states, are themselves intensional states, and so we are less worried, perhaps even rightly.) At any rate, I shall leave the restatement as it is until section III.5, where these difficulties are removed.

2. What kind of effect must S intend to produce in A if he is to mean something? What is intended by Grice's effect "which in some sense is within the control of the audience, or that in some sense of 'reason' the recognition of the intention behind x is for the audience a reason and not merely a cause" is any propositional or affective attitude or action. That actions and at least some propositional attitudes—notably believing—are intended by Grice is patent. That affective attitudes are to be included amongst the relevant sorts of effects is shown by Grice's willingness to allow that one meant something where the effect intended to be brought about by means of recognition of intention was that A should feel distressed, humiliated, offended, or insulted. So the phrase 'a certain response r' as it appears in the restatements below is equivalent to 'a certain propositional or affective attitude or action r'.

3. Thus, according to Grice, S meant something by uttering x only if S intended his utterance of x to produce a certain response r in a certain audience A. But if S is to mean something by uttering x, there are certain restrictions on the way he must intend to produce r in A. (1) S must intend to produce r in A "by means of" A's recognition of S's intention to produce r in A. And this involves the following. S utters x intending to produce r in A and intending that r be produced in A by virtue (at least in part) of A's belief that S uttered x intending to produce r in A. If we allow that reasons are causes, we may say that S intends r to be produced in A by virtue (at least in part) of A's belief that S uttered x intending to produce r in A just in case S uttered x intending that A's belief that S uttered x intending to produce r in A be (at least) a necessary part of a sufficient cause of A's response r. (2) The other restriction is that A's belief that S uttered x intending to produce r in A must not merely be intended to be a cause of A's response r, it must also be intended to be A's reason, or part of A's reason, for A's response r. (It is not diffi-

cult to see how the fact that S intends (or wants) A to do such-and-such may be a reason for A's doing such-and-such; it is perhaps more difficult to see how the fact that S intends A to think that such-and-such is the case may provide A with a reason for thinking that such-and-such is the case. What Grice primarily had in mind was simply this: sometimes the fact that a certain person believes (or believes he knows) a certain proposition to be true is good evidence that that proposition is true, and sometimes the fact that a certain person intends (or wants) another to believe that a certain proposition is true is good evidence that the former person himself believes (he knows) that that proposition is true. There are interesting questions concerning intentions, reasons, and affective attitudes, but for reasons that will be made apparent in section III.5, I shall ignore them.)

So we may, at this point, restate Grice's analysis of S-meaning in the following way.

S meant something by (or in) uttering x iff S uttered x intending

(1) that his utterance of x produce a certain response r in a certain audience A;

(2) that A recognize S's intention (1);

(3) that A's recognition of S's intention (1) shall function as at least part of A's reason for A's response r.[2]

5. We may further refine Grice's account of S-meaning by making explicit something which is implicit in his account but not built directly into his stated analysis of what it is for someone to mean something. If S is to mean something by uttering x, then S must intend A to recognize that S uttered x with the intention of producing thereby a certain response r in A. How will this recognition be achieved? It is implicit throughout Grice's article that S will utter x with the intention that A should recognize that x has a certain feature (or features) f, or that something f is true of x, and infer at least in part therefrom that S uttered x with the intention of producing r in A. In other words, if S meant something by uttering x, there is a certain feature (or features) f such that S uttered x intending that a certain audience A should recognize that x is f and intending that A should think, on the basis (in part) of thinking that x is f, that S uttered x intending to

----

produce a certain response r in A. For example: S utters 'It is raining' intending A to recognize that 'It is raining' has the feature of being an English sentence which means "it is raining" and intending A to infer (in part) therefrom that S uttered 'It is raining' intending thereby to produce in A the belief that it is raining, etc.; S utters 'urf' intending A to recognize that 'urf' has the feature of resembling the barking sound made by dogs and intending A to infer (in part) therefrom that S uttered 'urf' intending A to think that there are dogs nearby, etc. We might say that in the first example the relevant feature of S's utterance is a "non-natural" one, whereas in the second example it is a "natural" one.

Without this most recent emendation, Grice's analysis would seem to be open to some such counter-example as the following one. (That the counter-example is so recherché probably explains why the condition in question was not explicitly stated by Grice.)

S, a neuro-physiologist, knows that by giving A an electric shock of a certain sort he will effect a change in A's brain state *directly causing* A to believe that S administered the shock with the intention of producing in A the belief that A was about to inherit ten thousand acres of Mississippi swamp-land. Now even if S should administer this electric shock with the intention of getting A to believe, by means of recognition of intention, that he is about to inherit the swamp-land, I do not think we should want to say that by administering the shock S meant that A was about to inherit ten thousand acres of Mississippi swamp-land (or anything else). And I suggest that at least one thing which precludes this case from being an instance of S-meaning is that S did not administer the shock with the intention that A should *infer* (at least in part) from the fact that S administered the shock that S administered the shock with the intention of getting A to think he was about to inherit the swamp-land. For suppose that S and A had arranged that the electric shock should be used as a signal to inform A of the outcome of his grandmother's will; in this case one would not be reluctant to say that S meant something by administering the shock.

The following restatement may stand as our final version of Grice's original account of S-meaning.

S meant something by (or in) uttering x iff S uttered x intending

(1) that x have a certain feature(s) f;

(2) that a certain audience A recognize (think) that x is f;

(3) that A infer at least in part from the fact that x is f that S uttered x intending (4):

(4) that S's utterance of x produce a certain response r in A;

(5) that A's recognition of S's intention (4) shall function as at least part of A's reason for his response r.[3]

6. One can know that S meant something without knowing what he meant. Given that S performed a Gricean act of S-meaning, how are we to determine what S meant? Here Grice suggests:

that to ask what [S] meant is to ask for a specification of the intended effect . . .[4]

Accordingly, we may complete Grice's account of S-meaning with the following addendum.

What S meant by uttering x is determined by and only by the value of 'r'.

There are two things to notice about this part of Grice's analysis. The first point is in connection with the idea that an account of S-meaning may be taken as primary and an account of utterance-type/token meaning provided in terms of this primary account, and that is that what is meant is not even in part determined, logically, by what is said, i.e., by the value of 'x'. For if what were meant were determined, even in part, by the meaning of x, then this would, on the face of it, render circular an account of what x means in terms of what is or would be meant by uttering x. To say this does not commit Grice to holding that one can say whatever one likes and mean thereby whatever one pleases to mean. One must utter x with the relevant intentions, and not any value of 'x' will be appropriate to this end: I could not in any ordinary circumstances request you to pass the salt by uttering 'The flamingoes are flying south early this year'. Much more will be said about this later. The second point to notice is that Grice's condition pertaining to what is meant does not provide a criterion for determining what S meant, but only a criterion for determining what must be determined if one is to determine what

---

[3] Previously I stated conditions (1)–(3) somewhat differently; I owe this more perspicuous way of stating them to Grice.

[4] "Meaning", p. 385.

S meant. However, it is clear that Grice would want to say (or would have in 1957) that if the intended response was the belief that *p*, then *S* meant that *p*, and if the intended response was *A*'s doing *X*, then *S* meant that *A* was to do *X*. (But what does *S* mean when the intended response is *A*'s feeling humiliated?)

What of the connection between *S*-meaning and the meaning of utterance types and tokens? Here Grice leaves us with two rough suggestions:

> '*x* meant something' is (roughly) equivalent to 'Somebody meant something by *x*',

and

> '*x* means (timeless) that so-and-so' might as a first shot be equated with some statement or disjunction of statements about what 'people' (vague) intend (with qualifications about recognition) to effect by *x*.

I hope that whatever truth is contained in these suggestions will be revealed in chapters V and VI.

There are two very general objections which have been made against Grice's implied suggestion that his account of *S*-meaning may be taken as primary, and an account of utterance-meaning provided in terms of it. Since these objections apply to any such attempt to take the concept of *S*-meaning as logically prior to the concept of utterance-meaning, it will be well to consider them briefly here before turning to a more thorough examination of Grice's account of *S*-meaning.

The first objection may be put thus: any adequate account of *S*-meaning will require that *S* have certain propositional attitudes if he is to mean something; but such attitudes are correctly analysed only as attitudes toward sentences.

I do not believe that psychological states such as believing and desiring are best analysed as being attitudes toward sentences. Indeed, I think this view false. However, since I cannot prove that this view is false, I will leave a discussion of this important issue for some other occasion. But assume that propositional attitudes are attitudes toward sentences. It would not follow from this that Grice's account of *S*-meaning (or any relevantly similar account) is false, nor would it show that an account of utterance-meaning in terms of such an account is false. The most that would follow, if it does follow, is that the concept of *S*-meaning is not logically prior to the concept of utterance-meaning and that an analysis of meaning along Gricean lines is in a peculiar way like a "closed curve in space".

It does not seem unreasonable to suppose that in some interesting sense there are certain propositional attitudes which one cannot have unless one has a language (beliefs *about* language are language-dependent in an uninteresting sense), and from this it follows that it is not unreasonable to suppose that there are certain things one cannot mean unless one has a language. Some philosophers believe that there are certain things one cannot mean unless one has a language and that this fact constitutes an objection to a Gricean account of meaning. This is the second objection I have in mind. Hence, Searle, in a point directed against Grice, suggests that:

unless one has a language one cannot request of someone that he, e.g., undertake a research project on the problem of diagnosing and treating mononucleosis in undergraduates in American universities.[5]

I do not know whether Searle's point is true, and if it is true, I do not know whether it is logically true or only contingently true. But even if it is true, why should it be taken as an objection to Grice's programme? I think the answer is that it is thought that the thesis in question entails another thesis, which might be formulated in the following way: there is at least one proposition p such that it is impossible for anyone to believe and, *a fortiori*, to mean that p unless there is an utterance type x such that x means "p". This being so, one could not easily say that x means "p" only if people do, would, or could mean that p by uttering x. (Searle apparently fails to realize that if this is a difficulty for Grice's theory, it is equally a difficulty for his own theory of speech acts.)

But the view that in order to mean certain things one must have a language may more plausibly be taken as committing one not to the above thesis but only to the following thesis, which is compatible with a Gricean approach to meaning and language.

There are certain propositional attitudes such that it is possible for agents to have them independently of having any language or any other conventional means of communication and such that

---

[5] John R. Searle, *Speech Acts*, p. 38.

once agents have these propositional attitudes, they will communicate with one another. Once agents begin to communicate with one another they will begin to develop a conventional system of communication. Once even a rudimentary "language" or conventional system of communication is possessed by a group of agents it will then become possible for them to have propositional attitudes which they could not otherwise have; and this will make it possible for them to communicate things which they could not otherwise communicate, which in turn will result in a more sophisticated "language", which in turn will make it possible for them to have propositional attitudes they could not otherwise have, and so on.

On this view, then, the fact (if it is a fact) that there are certain propositional attitudes one cannot have unless one has a language is no objection to a Gricean approach to meaning and language. Certain aspects of this view will be elaborated in chapter V.

II

TOWARD AN ACCOUNT OF
S-MEANING

Introduction

ONE way of finding out what meaning is is to see what meaning is not, and in this chapter I will be mainly concerned to discuss certain objections to Grice's account of S-meaning; objections, first, to the alleged sufficiency of Grice's conditions, and objections, lastly, to the alleged necessity of one of Grice's conditions. In between I will try to show, in part, what must be added to Grice's account in order to arrive at a set of conditions which are jointly sufficient for someone's meaning something by uttering *x*. The objections I discuss in this chapter do not exhaust those that can and have been made against Grice's account of S-meaning. Some of these objections will be dealt with in subsequent chapters.

I shall begin with the restatement of Grice's account given on pp. 12–13.

II.1 *Some objections to the alleged sufficiency of Grice's analysans*

(a) Here is a slightly more detailed version of a counter-example of Strawson's.[1]

S wants to get *A* to believe that the house *A* is thinking of buying is rat-infested. *S* decides to bring about this belief in *A* by taking into the house and letting loose a big fat sewer rat. For *S* has the following scheme. He knows that *A* is watching him and knows that *A* believes that *S* is unaware that he, *A*, is watching him. It is *S*'s intention that *A* should (wrongly) infer from the fact that *S* let the rat loose that *S* did so with the intention that *A* should arrive at the house, see the rat, and, taking the rat as "natural evidence", infer therefrom that the house is rat-infested. *S* further intends *A* to realize that given the nature of the rat's arrival, the existence of the rat cannot be taken as genuine or natural evidence that the house is rat-infested; but *S* knows

---

[1] P. F. Strawson, "Intention and Convention in Speech Acts", pp. 446–7.

that A will believe that S would not so contrive to get A to believe the house is rat-infested unless S had very good reasons for thinking that it was, and so S expects and intends A to infer that the house is rat-infested from the fact that S is letting the rat loose with the intention of getting A to believe that the house is rat-infested. Thus S satisfies the conditions purported to be necessary and sufficient for his meaning something by letting the rat loose: S lets the rat loose intending (4) A to think that the house is rat-infested, intending (1)–(3) A to infer from the fact that S let the rat loose that S did so intending A to think that the house is rat-infested, and intending (5) A's recognition of S's intention (4) to function as his reason for thinking that the house is rat-infested. But even though S's action meets these conditions, Strawson is clearly right in claiming that "this is clearly not a case of attempted *communication* in the sense which . . . Grice is seeking to elucidate" (op. cit., p. 447).

What feature of this example makes it a counter-example? Strawson suggests that a minimum further condition of S's trying to communicate with A is that "he should not only intend A to recognize his intention to get A to think that p, but that he should also *intend A to recognize his intention to get A to recognize his intention* to get A to think that p" (ibid.). If Strawson is right, it would appear that we must add to the revised set of conditions the further condition that S have the intention

(6) that A should recognize S's intention (3).

(b) Strawson is wary of claiming that even with this addition Grice's analysis provides sufficient conditions. Strawson's caution is, I believe, vindicated by the following counter-example.

S, who has a hideous singing voice, intends (4) to bring about A's leaving the room by singing "Moon Over Miami". Further, S intends (1)–(3) that A should recognize that S is singing "Moon Over Miami" and infer therefrom that S is doing this with the intention (4) of getting A to leave the room, and S also intends (6) that A recognize S's intention (3) that A recognize S's intention to get A to leave the room (for S wishes to show his disdain for A's being in the room). Now S intends that A will believe that S plans to get rid of A *by means of S's repulsive singing*, but S expects and intends (5) that A's reason for leaving the room will in fact be A's recognition of S's intention (4) to get him to leave the room. In other words, while A is intended to *think* that

S intends to get rid of *A* by means of the *repulsive singing*, *A* is really intended to have as his reason for leaving the fact that *S* wants him to leave.

I think it is clear that *S* should not be said to have meant by singing "Moon Over Miami" that *A* was to leave the room; nor should we say that there was something else that *S* meant. Following Strawson, it would seem that the way to exclude this counter-example is to add the condition that *S* have the intention

(7) that *A* should recognize *S*'s intention (5).

Putting all of this together, Grice's analysans will have grown on the suggested way of revision to the following not uncomplicated set of conditions:

> *S* meant something by (or in) uttering *x* iff *S* uttered *x* intending
>
> (1) that *x* have a certain feature(s) *f*;
> (2) that a certain audience *A* recognize that *x* is *f*;
> (3) that *A* infer at least in part from the fact *x* is *f* that *S* uttered *x* intending (4):
> (4) that *S*'s utterance of *x* produce a certain response *r* in *A*;
> (5) that *A*'s recognition of *S*'s intention (4) shall function as at least part of *A*'s reason for his response *r*;
> (6) that *A* recognize *S*'s intention (3);
> (7) that *A* recognize *S*'s intention (5).

In effect this restatement says that *S* meant something by uttering *x* just in case *S* uttered *x* intending *A* to recognize that *S* uttered *x* intending to produce a response *r* in *A* by means of *A*'s recognition of *S*'s intention to produce *r* in *A*; that is, not only must *S* utter *x* with the original complex Gricean intention, he must also intend *A* to recognize this.

It will be relevant to notice that there is more of a rationale for the addition of this further intention than its use to rule out a few recherché counter-examples. For, in general, *S* can utter *x* intending to produce a certain response *r* in *A* by means of *A*'s recognition of this intention *only if S* expects *A* to recognize that *S* intends to produce *r* in *A* by means of recognition of intention *or else S* intends to *deceive A* as to the means by which *S* intends to produce *r* in *A*. In other words, given that *S* intends to produce *r* in *A* by means of recognition of intention (in the relevant sense, of course) and given that S does not want to deceive A, then S must—on pain of not satisfying his primary intention to produce r in A—expect A to think that S intends A's reason (or part of his reason) for his response r to be the fact that S intends to produce r in A. I believe this can be shown to be so by the following argument. (For simplicity I use an example in which the intended response is A's thinking that p; the argument should, *mutatis mutandis*, apply to any other type of response for which A has reasons.)

(i) A necessary condition of one's doing an act with the intention of thereby bringing about some further effect or result is that one should think that one's doing that act will (or might—this qualification should be made throughout) be sufficient (in the circumstances) for the production of that effect. So if S intends A to think that S uttered x intending to get A to think that p, S must think that A thinks (or will think) that S thinks that his utterance of x will be sufficient in the circumstances for getting A to think that p. (ii) Since in general the only way of getting someone to think that p is to provide that person with a *reason* (not necessarily a good reason but something which will be taken as a good reason) for thinking that p, A will not, in general, think that S uttered x intending to get A to think that p unless A thinks that S thinks that his utterance x (or some product thereof—this qualification can be ignored) will be taken by A to be a reason for thinking that p. Consequently, given that S intends A to think that S uttered x intending to get A to think that p, S must think that A thinks (or will think) that S thinks that A will take S's utterance x as a reason for thinking that p. (For example, Herod presents Salome with the severed head of St. John the Baptist intending to inform her that St. John the Baptist is dead and also intending her to think that he intended to inform her that St. John the Baptist is dead. It was possible for Herod to have the intention to inform Salome that St. John the Baptist is dead because he knew that she knew that one could not live without one's head and because he knew that she would recognize the head on the charger as the head of St. John the Baptist. It was possible for Herod to intend Salome to recognize his first intention because he knew that she knew that he knew that she knew that one could not live without one's head and because he knew that she knew that he knew that she would recognize the head on the charger as being the head of St. John the Baptist.) (iii) In general, S will think that A will think that the fact that S uttered x is a reason for thinking that p only if S thinks that A has a certain belief(s) r which would warrant A's thinking that p on the basis (in part) of thinking that S uttered x. Strictly, it is only necessary that S think A has *some* belief or beliefs which would warrant his thinking that p on the basis of thinking that S uttered x. But ordinarily S will be justified in thinking A has some such belief only if S thinks that A has a *certain* belief(s) which would warrant A's thinking that p on the basis of thinking S uttered x. Since this is so, A will, in general, think that S uttered x intending thereby to provide A with a reason for thinking that p only if A thinks that there is a certain belief(s) such that S thinks both that A has (or will have) that belief(s) and that A thinks (or will think) that that belief(s) would warrant A's thinking that p on the basis of thinking that S uttered x. So if S utters x intending to get A to think that p, he will expect A to have a certain belief(s) r which will warrant A's thinking that p on the basis of thinking that S uttered x; and if S also intends A to think that S uttered x intending to get A to think that p, then S will expect A to think that S thinks that A has (or will have) a certain belief(s) r' (which may or may not be identical with r) which will warrant A's thinking that p on the basis of thinking S uttered x. There are, then, *in principle*, two possibilities open to S if he utters x intending to produce in A the belief that p by means of A's recognition of this intention: (1) S will expect A to think that S intends part of A's reason for thinking that p to be the fact that S uttered x intending to get A to think that p, or (2) S will expect A to think that S thinks that A will have some reason other than recognition of S's intention to get A to think that p as his reason for thinking that p on the basis of thinking S uttered x. In this second case there is an intended discrepancy between the warrant A is intended to have for thinking that p on the basis of thinking S uttered x and the warrant he is intended to think S expects him to have; i.e., in the second case S intends A to be deceived as to the means by which S intends to produce in A the belief that p. This is precisely the situation we have in each of the above two counter-examples (except, of course, that in the "Moon Over Miami" example the intended response is a practical one).

(c) Unfortunately, however, there is still room for a more subtle type of deception, and, as if conditions (1)–(7) were not torturous enough, here is a further counter-example, a variation on the last one, to show that we still do not have a set of jointly sufficient conditions.

This time *S* sings "Tipperary" with the intention (4) of getting *A* to leave the room; the intention (1)–(3) that *A* recognize *S*'s intention (4) as a result of *A*'s inference from the fact that *S* is singing "Tipperary"; and the intention (6) that *A* recognize *S*'s intention (3) (for he again wishes to show his disdain for *A*'s being in the room). *S* also intends (5) that *A*'s reason for leaving the room will be his recognition of *S*'s intention (4). However, at this point *S* has the following plan. He intends that *A* should (wrongly) think that *S* intends *A* to think that *S* intends to get rid of *A* by means of *S*'s repulsive singing, but that *S* really intends to get rid of *A* by means of *A*'s recognition of *S*'s intention (4) to get *A* to leave. In other words, *S* intends *A* to reason as follows: "*S* intends me to think that he intends to get rid of me by means of his repulsive singing, but I recognize that he really intends my reason for leaving to be the fact that he wants to get rid of me and not, as he would falsely have me think, the fact that I can't stand his singing."

In the "Moon Over Miami" example there was an intended discrepancy between the reason *A* was intended to have for leaving and the reason *A* was intended to think he was intended to have. In the "Tipperary" example, *A* is intended to *think* (wrongly) that there is such an intended discrepancy. One might say here there is an intended discrepancy between the reason *A* was intended to think he was intended to have for leaving and the reason he was intended to think he was intended to think he was intended to have! (One might, as Grice has, question the possibility of this case being realized.[2] For how could *S* reasonably expect such a complicated inference to be made from the fact that he is singing 'Tipperary'? No doubt such cases require somewhat special circumstances, but this is no objection to their being counter-examples. The "special circumstances" appropriate for the "Tipperary" example might be this: after singing "Moon Over Miami" *S* has a third person, *B*, tell *A* *S*'s scheme in singing "Moon Over Miami", *B* pretending all the while to be secretly telling this behind *S*'s back. Thus, when *S* sings "Tipperary" *A* infers, *as intended*, that *S* is singing "Tipperary" with the same intentions he had in singing "Moon Over Miami".)

[2] H. P. Grice, "Utterer's Meaning and Intentions", p. 158.

It is clear that *S*'s scheme entails that *S* intend (7) that *A* recognize *S*'s intention (5), but I think that it is almost as clear that we should not want to say that *S* meant something by singing "Tipperary". Prima facie it might seem that the way to eliminate this type of counter-example would be to add a condition requiring *S* to intend

(8) that *A* recognize *S*'s intention (7);

but *in principle* we could keep on constructing counter-examples of the above kind, each time requiring us to add a condition of the above nature. If we grant that the only way of eliminating such counter-examples is to keep adding conditions which require *S* to have some (*n*)th-order intention that *A* recognize *S*'s (*n*−1)th-order intention, then this would seem to justify the fear expressed by Strawson that the analysis of *S*-meaning may involve an infinitely or indefinitely regressive series of intentions that intentions should be recognized. One who thinks that there are Gricean acts of communication and that the analysis of such acts does involve a regressive series of intentions will also think that this regress must be harmless. Such considerations are not likely to move a non-believer.

Grice has argued that there is no infinitely or indefinitely regressive series of intentions that intentions be recognized, harmless or otherwise.[3] For, Grice suggests, there will come a point in the purported regress, i.e. some purported (*n*)th-order intention that *A* recognize *S*'s (*n*−1)th-order intention, such that it will be known by *S* to be impracticably difficult for *A* to infer from the fact that *S* uttered *x* that *S* uttered *x* with an (*n*−1)th-order intention; and since one cannot, in general, intend to bring about a result one knows one cannot bring about, it follows that there will be some (*n*−1)th-order intention in the alleged regress such that *S* cannot have a further (*n*)th-order intention that *A* recognize *S*'s (*n*−1)th-order intention. The reason Grice offers for thinking that the alleged regress must reach a point beyond which ordinary, non-supersubtle mortals cannot proceed is based upon the increasing complexity of the counter-examples which seem to force the addition of conditions (6)–(8). For even if one can construct a further workable counter-example of the above type which shows that *S* must intend (9) that *A* recognize *S*'s intention (8), it is clear that one will soon come to a counter-example

---

[3] Ibid.

of this type where the calculations required to bring it off are simply too complicated to be made. It may not be precisely clear where this "cut-off" point lies (i.e. how many conditions requiring S to intend the recognition of some "lower-order" intention will be deemed necessary before the analysans is immune from a further counter-example of this type) but, Grice suggests, there will be *some* such cut-off point, and at that point one will have arrived at a set of conditions which are jointly sufficient and separately necessary for S meaning something by uttering x.

I have several objections to Grice's argument.

(1) Grice's reason for thinking that the alleged regress must reach a point beyond which it will be impracticably difficult to proceed is that there will come such a point in the construction of counter-examples of the above type. In other words, that there will come such a point in the construction of *counter-examples* is supposed to show that there will come such a point in *all* cases of communication.

I do not think this argument will do. Granted that the inferences and calculations required of A to some intention of S in uttering x in such complicated cases of *deception* as the above are extremely difficult. Nevertheless, it does not follow from this that the "inference" to a corresponding intention of S will also be difficult to make in the standard case of communication, where there is no deception and where everything is out in the open. To see that this assumption is false, one need only compare the difficulty A will have in inferring from the fact that S is singing "Tipperary" that S intends A's reason for leaving to be that S intends A to leave with the analogous inference in a straightforward case where S simply tells A to leave by uttering the sentence 'Leave the room!'

But suppose that Grice is right and that the purported regress does not arise, *for the reasons given by Grice*, and that, therefore, there will be some (n)th-order intention that A recognize S's ($n-1$)th-order intention such that S's (n)th intention is required as a necessary condition for S meaning something by uttering x in order to rule out some "Tipperary"-type counter-example and such that an ($n-1$)th-order intention is the "uppermost" intention anyone could possibly hope to be recognized. We can then make two further objections.

(2) Whatever S's (n)th intention is, it will be a *de facto* stopping point, one determined by the intelligence, ingenuity, and subtlety of actual people. But surely it is always possible to imagine two

people, a bit more intelligent and a bit more subtle than anyone else, who can succeed in bringing off a "Tipperary"-type inference requiring an $(n+1)$th-order intention to be added to the analysans. Therefore, even if Grice's argument to show that there is no regress is correct, the purported stopping point will not yield a set of logically sufficient conditions, which is what his analysans is meant to provide.

(3) Grice's argument rests on the assumption that the "cut-off" point (and, *a fortiori*, the final necessary condition of the analysans) is determined in the following way. First, determine the most complicated counter-example it is possible for any two people to bring off. In this example *S* will have some (n)th-order intention that *A* recognize *S*'s $(n-1)$th-order intention but no $(n+1)$th-order intention that *A* recognize *S*'s (n)th-order intention. To rule out this "uppermost" counter-example add a condition requiring *S* to have an $(n+1)$th-order intention that *A* recognize *S*'s (n)th-order intention. But, if Grice's reason for thinking the regress must reach a "cut-off" point is correct, then the $(n-1)$th-order intention of *S* in this "uppermost" counter-example will be the "uppermost" intention anyone could possibly hope to be recognized. Therefore, if we make it a necessary condition—in order to rule out this counter-example—that *S* have an $(n+1)$th-order intention that *A* recognize *S*'s (n)th-order intention that *A* recognize *S*'s $(n-1)$th-order intention, it will follow that a necessary condition of *S* meaning something by uttering *x* is that he intend *A* to recognize an intention he could not possibly expect *A* to recognize; so if we take this way out it will be impossible for anyone to mean anything. On the other hand, if we only require that *S* intend *A* to recognize *S*'s $(n-1)$th-order intention, then, not only will this necessarily fail to rule out at least one counter-example (and so not be sufficient), it will have the consequence that only the two most subtle and intelligent beings alive could mean anything, and they could only communicate with one another. (Grice has suggested that one way of avoiding this last objection would be to have the analysans "vary from case to case, depending on such things as the nature of the intended response, the circumstances in which the attempt to elicit the response is made, and the intelligence of the utterer and of the audience" (ibid., p. 159). But even Grice admits that it is doubtful whether this would be acceptable; and even if this way out were accepted, I fear it might still have the consequence that *S* will

always be required to have *some* intention which he does not think *A* could recognize and which is necessary for his meaning something in the circumstances, and so *A* could never (except, perhaps, where *S* miscalculated) know that *S* meant something.)

What makes each of the examples (a)–(c) a counter-example is that *S* intends to deceive *A* in one way or another. It might be thought that these counter-examples could be eliminated without involving a proliferation of intentions by requiring that *S not* have certain intentions. Grice has suggested the possibility that instead of eliminating the above counter-examples by the addition of conditions (6)–(8), we add instead to the analysans a condition requiring it to be the case that:

there is no inference-element *E* such that [*S*] uttered *x* intending both (1′) that *A*'s determination of *r* should rely on *E* and (2′) that *A* should think [*S*] to intend that (1′) be false. (Ibid.)

(It is clear from the context in which this appears that '*A*'s determination of *r*' means (roughly) the same as 'the inference (theoretical or practical) by which *A* reaches his response *r*'.)

I have my doubts as to whether this condition is necessary;[4] more importantly, I fail to see how it eliminates all of the counter-examples it was designed to eliminate. In the "Moon Over Miami" example, for instance, it is true that *S* intends *A*'s belief that *S* wants *A* to leave to be an "inference-element" in *A*'s practical inference and true that *S* intends that *A* think that *S* does not intend *A*'s belief that *S* wants *A* to leave to be an "inference-element" in *A*'s practical inference; nevertheless, there is no reason to suppose that *A* thinks (or was intended to think) that *S* intends *A not* to have his belief that *S* wants him to leave as an "inference-element" in his determination to leave: this example would still be a counter-example if *A* thought (and was intended to think) that *S* sang "Moon Over Miami" not caring in the least if *A* left because *S* wanted him to leave but simply expecting that a bit of repulsive singing would be more effective.

I will not attempt to construct a more effective condition of this type, for I think that no condition requiring *S* not to have certain intentions will adequately deal with the problems raised by the preceding counter-examples. But before offering what I

---

[4] It follows from what I say in section II. 3 that this condition cannot be a necessary condition.

think is a solution to those problems, I should like to consider one more alleged counter-example, one put forward by John Searle.[5]

(d) An American soldier (*S*) is captured during World War II by Italian troops (*A*). *S* would like to get *A* to believe he is a German officer by telling them in German or Italian that he is a German officer, but he knows neither language. However, *S* does remember a line from a German poem he memorized in school, and, hoping *A* does not know German, he utters the sentence, 'Kennst du das Land, wo die Zitronen blühen?' ('Knowest thou the land where the lemon trees bloom?') with the intention of deceiving *A* into thinking that he is saying in German "I am a German officer".

Thus, *S* utters the sentence 'Kennst . . .' intending

(1) that 'Kennst . . .' be a German sentence (*f*);
(2) that *A* recognize that 'Kennst . . .' is a German sentence;
(3) that *A* infer at least in part from the fact that *S* uttered a German sentence that *S* uttered 'Kennst . . .' intending (4):
(4) that *S*'s utterance of 'Kennst . . .' produce in *A* the belief that *S* is a German officer;
(5) that *A*'s recognition of *S*'s intention (4) shall function as part of *A*'s reason for believing that *S* is a German officer;

and since there is no reason why *S* should not want *these* intentions recognized, or even recognized that they are intended to be recognized, we may consider him to have intentions (6) and (7) too. Nevertheless, I think one feels that it would be wrong, or at least not quite right, to say that *S* meant that he was a German officer (or anything else) by uttering 'Kennst . . .'.

Searle's explanation of what precludes this case from being an instance of *S*-meaning is this:

> We have here a case where I am trying to produce a certain effect by means of the recognition of my intention to produce that effect, but the device I use to produce this effect is one which is conventionally, by the rules governing the use of that device, used as a means of producing quite different illocutionary effects.[6]

[5] "What is a Speech Act?", pp. 229–30; *Speech Acts*, p. 44.
[6] "What is a Speech Act?", p. 230.

This explanation will not do. At a boring party Miss *S* might say to her escort, Mr. *A*, 'Don't you have to inspect the lemon trees early in the morning?', and mean thereby that she wants to leave.

What, if anything, makes Searle's example a counter-example? Strictly speaking, Searle's example is under-described, and it is possible that the American soldier uttered 'Kennst . . .' intending his Italian audience to reason (roughly) in either of the following two ways. (i) " 'Kennst . . .' is a German sentence. *S* knows (or should know) that we do not speak German and knows that we know he knows this. But given the fact that he uttered a German sentence in these circumstances he is most likely uttering a sentence which means "I am a German officer" in German with the intention that we should infer that he intends to inform us that he is a German officer simply in virtue of the fact that he uttered a German sentence in these circumstances." However, I think the more likely interpretation of the soldier's scheme is that he intended his audience to reason: (ii) "*S* uttered 'Kennst . . .'. This is a German sentence. The fact that he uttered a German sentence shows that he thinks or hopes we understand German. So he must intend us to recognize, in virtue of our knowledge of German, what the sentence means and to infer from this what he meant by uttering it. . . . Well, given the preceding and the circumstances, it is most likely that 'Kennst . . .' means the same as 'I am a German officer' and that *S*'s intention in uttering this is to inform us that he is a German officer."

If we think of the American soldier as intending his captors to reason in the way characterized in (i), then I think it will not be incorrect to say that he did mean that he was a German officer. For in this event Searle's example will not differ relevantly from the following example of Grice's, where, I believe, we should want to say that something was meant.

A Port Said prostitute, lounging seductively in a shady doorway, utters in ingratiating tones an Arabic sentence which means "You filthy pig of a sailor" with the intention of picking up a British sailor.[7]

Unlike Searle's example, we are here inclined to say that the prostitute did mean something by uttering the Arabic sentence, and this suggests that the relevant difference between the two

---

[7] A bowdlerized version of this example is in "Utterer's Meaning and Intentions", p. 162.

cases, and the difference which accounts for our differing intuitions about the two cases, is that the soldier intended his captors to reason in the way characterized in (ii). There are at least two possibly relevant respects in which (ii) differs from (i).

(1) In both cases S utters x intending A to think *falsely* that x has a certain feature f' (that 'Kennst . . .' means "I am a German officer"), but it is only in (ii) that S intends A to have this false belief that x is f' as part of his reason for thinking that S uttered x intending to produce a response r in A (etc.).

But that this is *not* a sufficient condition for S not meaning something by uttering x is shown, I believe, by the following example. S's wife, a present-day Mrs. Malaprop, confuses the words 'erotic' and 'erratic' so that she believes that 'erotic' means "erratic" and that 'erratic' means "erotic". S would like to tell his wife not to order his buttermilk from the milkman, because the milkman is too erratic. Rather than begin a futile explanation or use several words instead of one, S takes the easy way out and utters the sentence, 'Dear, please don't order my buttermilk from the milkman; he's too erotic'.

I do not think one would be at all disinclined to say that S here meant something and that what he meant by uttering 'he's too erotic' was that the milkman was too erratic, and this despite the fact that A was intended to have the false belief about the meaning of 'erotic' as her basis for inferring what S meant from what S uttered.

(2) I believe that what does make Searle's example a counterexample is this: S utters x intending A to think that x has a certain feature f (that 'Kennst . . .' is a German sentence) and intending A to think (wrongly)—on the basis of thinking x is f— that S uttered x intending A to think that x has a certain feature f' (that 'Kennst . . .' means "I am a German officer") and intending A to think—*on the basis of A's thinking that x is f'*—that S uttered x intending to produce a response r in A (etc.). In other words, there is an intended discrepancy between *the basis* A *is intended to have* for thinking S uttered x intending to produce r in A and *the basis A is intended to think he is intended to have* for thinking S uttered x intending to produce r in A. (In the "Mrs. Malaprop" example there is no such discrepancy: the belief that 'erotic' means "erratic" is both the basis A is intended to have and the basis A is intended to think A is intended to have, and so on.)

It will be to no avail to revise Grice's definition by requiring S to intend A to recognize that S intends A to infer S's intentions in uttering x from the fact that x has a certain feature(s) f; for we could then construct a further counter-example in which there is an intended discrepancy between the basis A is intended to think he is intended to have and the basis A is intended to think he is intended to think he is intended to have. For despite first appearances, Searle's example is a counter-example of the same type as the preceding three.

II.2 *Mutual knowledge* *

I should now like to argue that there is a very common, ordinary feature of our everyday life, one which has to do with interpersonal knowledge, which once noticed will provide us with a condition which is at once a necessary condition for performing an act of communication and a condition which will eliminate those counter-examples based on deception without, I think, entailing a regressive series of intentions that "lower-order" intentions be recognized; although, as we will see, it does entail a quite harmless regress of the sort involved in knowing that one knows that p.

The phenomenon I am alluding to has no name, nor is there an otherwise simple way of referring to it. For this reason I shall coin the barbarism "mutual knowledge*", and I shall speak of two people, S and A, mutually knowing* that p, or of it being mutually known* that p by S and A, and so on; it will later be clear that any number of people greater than two may also mutually know* that p.

(a) *Definition of 'S and A mutually know* that p'*.

For convenience, let

$\quad$ '$K^*_{SA}p$' = df. 'S and A mutually know* that p'.

We can now say

$\quad K^*_{SA}p$ iff
$\quad K_S p$ [S knows that p]
$\quad K_A p$
$\quad K_S K_A p$
$\quad K_A K_S p$
$\quad K_S K_A K_S p$
$\quad K_A K_S K_A p$

$$K_S K_A K_S K_A p$$
$$K_A K_S K_A K_S p$$

.

.

.

(b) *Example.* Suppose that you and I are dining together and that we are seated across from one another and that on the table between us is a rather conspicuous candle. We would therefore be in a situation in which I am facing the candle and you, and you are facing the candle and me. (Consequently, a situation in which *S* is facing the candle and *A*, who is facing the candle and *S*, who is facing the candle and *A*, who is facing the candle and *S*, who is facing . . .) I submit that were this situation to be realized, you and I would mutually know* that there is a candle on the table.

Let us pretend that we are now in the situation described. Clearly, I know that there is a candle on the table. So

$$K_S p.$$

I also know that you know that there is a candle on the table. How do I know this? First, I know that if a "normal" person (i.e., a person with normal sense faculties, intelligence, and experience) has his eyes open and his head facing an object of a certain size (etc.), then that person will see that an object of a certain sort is before him. Secondly, I know that you are a "normal" person and I see that your open-eyed head is facing the candle. (This is not intended to be overly exact.) So

$$K_S K_A p.$$

Further, I do not presume to be the only person aware of the above-mentioned law about normal people in certain circumstances; I also know that you know that normal people see things that are in their line of vision when their eyes are open, etc. And I have seen that you see that my open-eyed head is facing the candle. So I know that you know that I know that there is a candle on the table; i.e.,

$$K_S K_A K_S p.$$

Just as I know that you know the relevant law about normal observers, so I know you have just the same type of grounds for knowing that I know it, too. And since I see that you see my head facing your head which has the candle in its line of vision, I know that you know that I know that you know that there is a candle on the table. So

$$K_S K_A K_S K_A p.$$

I could go on now to construct a further step which illustrates that for the same reason that I am justified in thinking that $K_A K_S K_A p$, so you have the same reason, *mutatis mutandis*, for thinking that $K_S K_A K_S p$, which would show, of course, that

$$K_S K_A K_S K_A K_S p;$$

but there is, I trust, no need to do this, for at this point it should be clear (i) that I can go on like this forever; (ii) that this regress is perfectly harmless; and (iii) that the phenomenon which obtains in this case is a general one: it will obtain, broadly speaking, whenever S and A know that p, know that each other knows that p, and all of the relevant facts are "out in the open".

(c) *Conditions for mutual knowledge**. Not quite so roughly, I think one can account for the possibility of mutual knowledge* and the conditions which must obtain for it to be realized in something like the following way.

First, I think that, in general, for any person x and any proposition p, if x knows that p, then there is a property H such that x knows that x is H and such that being H is sufficient for knowing that p, being H is sufficient for knowing that being H is sufficient for knowing that p, and so on;

i.e., $(x)\ (p)\ (Kxp \rightarrow (\exists H)\ (KxHx\ \&\ (y)\ (Hy \rightarrow Kyp\ \&\ Ky(z)$
$(Hz \rightarrow Kzp)\ \&\ Ky(z)\ (Hz \rightarrow Kz(w)\ (Hw \rightarrow Kwp))\ \&\ Ky(z)$
$(Hz \rightarrow Kz(w)\ (Hw \rightarrow Kw(v)\ (Hv \rightarrow Kvp)))\ \&\ \ldots$

For example, all "normal" people know that snow is white, know that all normal people know that snow is white, know that all normal people know that all normal people know that snow is white, and so on *ad infinitum*. (Likewise, I should think, for all or most of our common general knowledge; so if S and A mutually know* that each is "normal", all of the general knowledge each has in virtue of being a "normal" person will also be mutually known* by them.) To take another example, Jones knows that there is a house in front of him; he knows that anyone else in a relevantly similar position will know that there is a house in front of him; he knows that anyone else in a relevantly similar position will know that anyone else in a relevantly similar position will know that there is a house in front of him, and so on.

This should not be surprising. In general, if one knows that p, one will know *how* one knows that p; indeed, in most cases in which one knows how one knows that p one would not know that p unless one knew how one knew that p; but knowing how one knows that p can be construed as just knowing that having a certain property is sufficient for anyone's knowing that p. Thus, when in such cases one knows that p, there is a property H such that one knows that being H is sufficient for knowing that p. But, in such cases, it will be in virtue of knowing that p that one knows that one knows that p because one is H, and so one will know that being H is sufficient for knowing that being H is sufficient for knowing that p; and so on. Now, since relevant property H has this power with respect to knowing that p by virtue of the fact that being H is sufficient for knowing that p, the preceding line of argument suggests another truth about properties which satisfy the above conditions, a truth which will shortly be useful, viz. : there are properties, let H be one, such that, for any proposition p, if being H is sufficient for knowing that p, then being H is sufficient for knowing that being H is sufficient for knowing that p; i.e., $(\exists H)\,(p)\,((x)\,(Hx \to Kxp) \to (y)\,(Hy \to Ky(z)\,(Hz \to Kzp)))$.

Given the above, we can account for how it is that we mutually know* that there is a candle on the table. (No doubt we would mutually know* that each of us is "normal" before we got to the table, but for present purposes I shall pretend this is not the case.)

First, all "normal" people know that if a normal person has his eyes open and his head facing an object of a certain type (etc.), that person will know that an object of that type is before him; all normal people know that all normal people know this; and so on.

Second, all "normal" people know that anyone who appears and/or behaves in a certain way Ψ is normal; all normal people know that all normal people know this; and so on.

Now in the above example we have a situation in which, *ex hypothesi*, it is the case that

(1) S is (visibly) ψ and facing the candle and A;
(2) A is (visibly) ψ and facing the candle and S.

From this, together with the preceding two assumptions, it follows (once we fill in the obvious details) that S and A mutually know* that there is a candle on the table.

A situation in which two people are face-to-face with one another and the fact that p is a paradigm of mutual knowledge*, if anything is, but to labour, I hope, the obvious, it is not the only type of situation which generates mutual knowledge*. In particular, two people might mutually know* that p even though they are not directly acquainted with one another and even though they each have entirely different grounds for thinking that p. Thus, two people who have never met but who know of each other may reasonably assume that they mutually know* that London is a city in England; it might be mutually known* by S and A that S is in pain because it is mutual knowledge* that S is behaving in a certain way; or, to take an example closer to home, since S and A mutually know* that S uttered the sentence 'Please pass the salt', they mutually know* that S uttered 'Please pass the salt' intending that A should pass the salt because S wants him to.

In each case of mutual knowledge* we have a finitely describable situation such that in virtue of certain general features of this situation it follows that two people have an infinite amount of knowledge about each other. We ought, then, to be able to state a set of conditions which are such that S and A will mutually know* that p just in case these conditions are satisfied. The above discussion suggests that we might capture just those general conditions which generate mutual knowledge* in the following way. First, allow that it is a truth about knowledge in general that, for any property H and any proposition q, if one knows that whoever is H knows that q, and if one knows of any particular person that he is H, then one knows that that person knows that q; i.e., $(x)\,(H)\,(q)\,(z)\,((Kx(y)\,(Hy \rightarrow Kyq)\; \&\; KxHz) \rightarrow KxKzq)$. We may now say that

S and A mutually know* that p iff there are properties F and G such that

(1) S is F;
(2) A is G;
(3) both being F and being G are sufficient for knowing

that p, that S is F, and that A is G; i.e., $(x)\,(Fx \text{ v } Gx \to Kxp$
& $KxFS$ & $KxGA)$;

(4) for any proposition q, if both being F and being G are sufficient for knowing that q, then both being F and being G are sufficient for knowing that both being F and being G are sufficient for knowing that q; i.e., $(q)\,((x)$ $(Fx \text{ v } Gx \to Kxq) \to (y)\,(Fy \text{ v } Gy \to Ky(z)\,(Fz \to Kzq)$ & $Ky(w)\,(Gw \to Kwq)))$.

These conditions are fairly abstract. Here is how they might be instantiated in an actual case of mutual knowledge*, for instance our "candle" example. In that example, let $F =$ the property of being an object x such that x is a visibly "normal", open-eyed, conscious person who is identical with S and who, at a close distance, is directly facing the candle and A, who is a visibly "normal", open-eyed, conscious person who is directly facing the candle and S; and let $G =$ the property of being an object x such that x is a visibly "normal", open-eyed, conscious person who is identical with A and who, at a close distance, is directly facing the candle and S, who is a visibly "normal", open-eyed conscious person who is directly facing the candle and A. Now, *ex hypothesi*, S is F and A is G, and I submit that by virtue of their respectively possessing properties F and G, both S and A know that there is a candle on the table, that S is F and that A is G. With respect to the satisfaction of condition (4), I have already argued that generally when there is knowledge there is some property H such that, for any proposition q, if being H is sufficient for knowing that q, then being H is sufficient for knowing that being H is sufficient for knowing that q. I suggest that if any properties are of this sort, properties F and G are; and to get from here to the desired conclusion that condition (4) is satisfied, I suggest the following principle: if two properties entail just the same purely general properties, and if both properties are such that, for any proposition p, it is true of each property that if it is sufficient for knowing that p, then it is sufficient for knowing that it is sufficient for knowing that p, then, for any proposition q, if either property is sufficient for knowing that q, then the one is sufficient for knowing that the other is sufficient for knowing that q. Thus, we may conclude that, for any proposition q, if both being F and being G are sufficient for knowing that q, then both being F and being G are sufficient for knowing that both being F and being G are sufficient for knowing that q; for, roughly put, the two properties do not differ relevantly, since S and A share all of the purely general properties entailed by either F or G.

(d) *Prima facie objections.* I think one would be hard put to find reasons why in the "candle" example I could not go on indefinitely in the way specified. But even granting this there are two objections which might be made.

(1) "What follows from the example is not that S and A mutually know* that there is a candle on the table, but only that by proceeding in the above way each is capable of *acquiring* an indefinite amount of knowledge of the kind specified."

(2) "Even if S and A *now* mutually know* that there was a candle on the table, it doesn't follow that they knew this before it was *pointed out* to them that they could go on indefinitely in the way indicated."

I will not attempt to answer these objections conclusively; but I think I can remove a good part of the motivation behind them by calling attention to the following two facts. First, it is no objection to the claim that S knows that p that the thought that p never once entered S's head. For example, I trust that it is true of each philosophy don in Oxford that he knows that his maternal grandmother was never married to Benito Mussolini. Second, it is no objection to the claim that S knows A knows S knows A knows S knows that p that S may have to be "convinced" or "brought to see" that he is entitled to claim to know this. I doubt that many a non-philosopher would agree right off the bat that he knows that he knows that he knows that $843 + 2 = 845$. Moreover, if having to be "brought to see" that p is sufficient for defeating the claim that S knows that p, then this will be embarrassing in general for a Gricean account of communication. For a good deal of arguing is often needed to show someone that his intention in uttering 'Shut the door!' was to get his audience to shut the door by means of recognition of this intention.

(e) *A revised analysans.* In Strawson's example it is not mutually known* by S and A that S uttered x, and so not mutually known* by S and A that S uttered x intending to produce r in A by means of recognition of intention. In the "Moon Over Miami" and "Tipperary" examples it is mutually known* by S and A that S uttered x but not mutually known* by them that S uttered *x* intending to produce *r* in *A* by means of recognition of this intention. In Searle's example it is not mutual knowledge* that intends his utterance *x* to be evidence that he uttered *x* intending to produce *r* in *A* by means of recognition of intention simply in virtue of *x* being a German sentence uttered in the circumstances.

In the standard or paradigm case of Gricean communication it is mutually known* by *S* and *A* that *S*'s utterance *x* has a certain feature(s) *f* and mutually known* that the fact that *S*'s utterance *x* is *f* (together with certain other facts) is conclusive evidence that *S* uttered *x* intending to produce a response *r* in *A* by means of recognition of this intention and conclusive evidence that *S* uttered *x* intending it to be mutual knowledge* that *S*'s utterance *x* is conclusive evidence that *S* uttered *x* intending to produce *r* in *A* by means of recognition of this intention.

This is what should be expected just on the basis of the fact that by making sure everything is out in the open *S* increases his chances of securing his primary intention. But I believe that we can say something even stronger: given that *S* has no intention of deceiving *A*, *S* can, in general, utter *x* intending to produce a certain response *r* in *A* by means of *A*'s recognition of this intention *only if S* expects it to be mutually known* by *S* and *A* that *S* uttered *x* intending to produce *r* in *A* by means of recognition of this intention.

In section II. 1(b) I argued that given that *S* does not intend to deceive *A* and given that *S* utters *x* intending to produce a response *r* in *A* by means of *A*'s recognition of this intention, *S* can expect *A* to think that *S* uttered *x* intending to produce *r* in *A only if S* expects *A* to think *S* intends to produce *r* in *A* by means of recognition of this intention. Grant that this is so, and suppose that *S* utters *x* intending to produce *r* in *A* by means of recognition of intention and that *S* has no intention to deceive *A*. Given, then, that *S* uttered *x* with the complex Gricean intention, he must think that *A* will (or might) think that *S* uttered *x* intending to produce *r* in *A* by means of recognition of this intention. But *A* knows that a necessary condition of *S* uttering *x* intending to produce *r* in *A* by means of recognition of this intention is that *S* expects *A* to think that *S* uttered *x* intending to produce *r* in *A* by means of recognition of intention. So *A* will not think that *S* uttered *x* intending to produce *r* in *A* by means of recognition of intention unless *A* thinks that *S* thinks that *A* thinks that *S* uttered *x* intending to produce *r* in *A* by means of recognition of intention. S, knowing this is so, must thus think that A will think that S thinks that A will think that S uttered x intending to produce r in A by means of recognition of intention. A, knowing this is so, will not think that S uttered x intending to produce r in A by means of recognition of intention unless he thinks S thinks he thinks S thinks he thinks S uttered x intending to produce r in A by means of recognition of intention; and so on.

It might seem, then, that the way to revise Grice's analysans is to require that S utter x intending it to be mutually known* by S and A that the fact that S uttered x in the circumstances is evidence that S uttered x intending to produce a response r in A by means of recognition of this intention. But were we to revise the definition in this way we would still not have adequately dealt with the type of counter-example we are concerned to eliminate; for we would be open to a counter-example in which S utters x intending it to be mutually known* by S and A that the fact that S uttered x in the circumstances is evidence that S uttered x intending to produce r in A by means of recognition of intention, but also intending A to think that S intended it not to be mutual knowledge* that his utterance of x in the circumstanes was evidence that S uttered x intending to produce r in A by means of recognition of intention. For example, S might arrange bogus "evidence" that p knowing that A will disclose his presence to S while S is contriving the "evidence" and knowing that it will, in that event, be mutual knowledge* that the fact that S is contriving "evidence" that p is evidence that S is doing this with the same type of scheme he had when he was the subject of Strawson's counter-example (we may suppose, too, that S intends A to think that p on the basis of thinking S intends A to think that p, despite the disclosure); and so S and A will mutually know* (or believe*) that S intends to produce in A the belief that p by means of recognition of this intention on the basis of mutually knowing* (or believing*) that S was contriving bogus evidence that p; yet we should not want to say that S meant that p by contriving bogus evidence that p.

Nor will it do to revise Grice's definition by requiring S to intend it to be mutual knowledge* that the fact that S uttered x in the circumstances is evidence that he intended the fact that he uttered x in the circumstances to be mutually known* to be evidence that he uttered x intending to produce a response r in A by means of recognition of intention. For this leaves open the possibility of a counter-example in which S utters x with those intentions, but also intending A to think that S intended it not to be mutual knowledge* that the fact that S uttered x in the circumstances is evidence that he intended the fact that he uttered x in the circumstances to be mutually known* to be evidence that he uttered x intending to produce r in A by means of recognition of intention.

Most generally described, the problem seems to be this. So long as a proposed account of S-meaning requires S to have some intention i such that the analysans does not secure that it is impossible for S to intend A to think that S did not utter x with intention i, then the analysans will not be sufficient. In other words, if S is to mean something by uttering x, then all of the intentions necessary for his meaning something must be out in the open; there must be no possibility of "hidden" intentions which are constitutive of an act of meaning something.[8]

I suggest that at this stage we revise Grice's account of S-meaning in the following way.

> S meant something by (or in) uttering x iff S uttered x intending thereby to realize a certain state of affairs E which is (intended by S to be) such that the obtainment of E is sufficient for S and a certain audience A mutually knowing* (or believing*) that E obtains and that E is conclusive (very good or good) evidence that S uttered x intending

> (1) to produce a certain response r in A;
> (2) A's recognition of S's intention (1) to function as at least part of A's reason for A's response r;
> (3) to realize E.

A few comments may be helpful.

(1) Typically, E will essentially involve the fact that S, a person having such-and-such properties, uttered a token of type X having a certain feature(s) f in the presence of A, a person having such-and-such properties, in certain circumstances C. For instance, E might be, in part, the state of affairs which obtained when S uttered 'Please pass the salt' in the direction of A while they were dining together. From the fact that this state of affairs obtained we could reasonably conclude that S and A mutually knew* that it obtained and mutually knew* that the fact that this state of

---

[8] Cf. Strawson, "Intention and Convention in Speech Acts", p. 454.

affairs obtained was conclusive evidence that S uttered 'Please pass the salt' intending A to pass the salt because S wanted him to pass the salt and intending to realize the aforementioned state of affairs.

(2) It follows from the original Gricean account of what it is for S to mean something by uttering x that S meant something by uttering x only if S uttered x intending thereby to realize a certain state of affairs E' such that A would recognize that E' obtained and recognize (think) that E' is evidence that S uttered x intending to produce a response r in A. I have argued that S can non-deceptively utter x with the original complex Gricean intention only if S intends it to be mutually known* (or believed*) by S and A that S uttered x with the complex Gricean intention. A consequence of this is that S can non-deceptively utter x with the complex Gricean intention only if S utters x intending thereby to realize a certain state of affairs E' such that it will be mutually known* (or believed*) by S and A that E' obtains and mutually known* (or believed*) by them that E' is evidence that S uttered x intending to produce a certain response r in A by means of recognition of this intention. Now an argument of the same type as that used to show that, necessarily, if S utters x non-deceptively intending to produce a response r in A by means of recognition of intention, then S intends it to be mutually known* (or believed*) by S and A that S uttered x intending to produce r in A by means of recognition of intention can be given to show that A will not take E' as evidence that S intends to produce r in A by means of recognition of intention unless A thinks that S expected it to be mutually believed* by S and A that S uttered x intending to realize E' (for A will not, *ceteris paribus*, think E' is evidence that S uttered x intending to produce r in A (etc.) unless he thinks S intended to realize E'; so A knows that S will expect A to think that S intends to realize E'; so A knows that S will expect A to think that S will expect A to think that S intends to realize E' . . .). It follows, then, that either E' will be intended by S to be mutually believed* to be evidence that S uttered x intending to realize E' or else there will be some other state of affairs E'' which S also intends to realize and which S intends to be mutually believed* to be evidence that S uttered x intending to realize E'. If the first disjunct is the case, then we have the proposed definition; if the second disjunct is the case, then we have the proposed definition or a vicious regress.

(3) An intuitive reaction to the counter-examples based on deception is that what precludes these cases from being instances of S-meaning is that S does not utter x expecting that if the intentions with which he uttered x are satisfied, A will recognize that S meant something by uttering x. One's next reaction is likely to be to disregard one's first intuition; for to say that S meant something by uttering x only if S intended or expected A to recognize that S meant something by uttering x seems a bit too circular to be either right or perspicuous. The proposed redefinition is such that S cannot utter x with the requisite intentions without expecting it to be mutually known* (or believed*) by him and A that he did so, if the intentions with which he uttered x are satisfied; that is, S cannot mean something by uttering x without expecting that if the intentions with which he uttered x are satisfied, A will recognize that he meant something by uttering x. That this is so is secured by the fact that for any state of affairs E satisfying the definition and for any proposition q, if the obtainment of E is sufficient for S and A mutually knowing* that q, then the obtainment of E is sufficient for S and A mutually knowing* that S uttered x believing that the obtainment of E would be sufficient for S and A mutually knowing* that q. So the proposed redefinition has the merit of confirming one's original intuition without being circular.

(4) I do not think that the mutual knowledge* condition commits S to having an infinite number of intentions, since one may intend *all* the consequences of one's act without intending *each* consequence. However, even if the definition did entail an infinitely regressive series of intentions, I do not think that this would be an objection to the definition; for the concept of mutual knowledge* would enable us to see why such a regress would be harmless and why such a regress would not preclude us from providing sufficient conditions for an instance of S-meaning.

(5) Does the definition allow S to utter x without actually intending to produce r in A? The notion of "good evidence" as it occurs in the definition is to be understood in its epistemic sense, and this entails that S cannot think that E is good evidence that he intends to produce r in A if he knows that he does not have this intention. Now I think that the sort of intention relevant to the definition is such that for any intention of this sort, S knows whether or not he has that intention. It follows that if S

does not have a certain intention, then he knows that he does not have that intention; and it follows from this that if *S* does not know that he does not have a certain intention, then he has that intention. We may conclude, then, that if *S* intends *E* to be good evidence that he intends to produce *r* in *A*, then he intends to produce *r* in *A*. However, should this line of argument ultimately prove unacceptable, we could easily circumvent the need for it by directly stipulating in the definition that *S* has those intentions which he intends *E* to be good evidence that he has.

Even if it is granted that the revisions made so far are both necessary and sufficient for dealing with those counter-examples based on deception, there are at least three different and further respects in which the most recently revised analysans (and, of course, Grice's original analysans) does not provide a set of jointly sufficient conditions for *S* meaning something by uttering *x*. The objections alluded to will be encountered and dealt with in the next chapter, when I formulate my own account of *S*-meaning.

II.3 *Some objections to the alleged necessity of Grice's analysans*

The central condition in Grice's analysis, the condition which gives the Gricean account of *S*-meaning much of its force and originality, is that to mean something is to intend to produce a certain response in an audience *by means of the audience's recognition of one's intention to produce that response*. In this section I hope to point out that there are standard instances of *S*-meaning where *S* does utter *x* intending to produce a certain response *r* in *A*, but where it is no part of *S*'s intention that part of *A*'s reason for his response *r* be that *S* intends to produce *r* in *A*. Pointing this out will show, in effect, that while the condition that *S* intend to produce *r* in *A* *by means of recognition of this intention* is perhaps a necessary condition for performing an act of "telling"—either "telling" *A* that such-and-such is the case or "telling" *A* to do such-and-such—it is not a necessary condition for *S* meaning something by uttering *x*.

(a) If Grice's account of what it is for someone to mean something were correct, an unwelcome and somewhat ironic consequence would be that although Grice will have written and published an article of several pages on what it is for someone to mean something, Grice will have meant almost nothing by what he wrote. For although Grice's primary intention in writing his paper was to induce in us certain beliefs (albeit of a "conceptual" nature) about meaning, he neither expected nor intended that our reason for believing that what he wrote is true would be the fact that he intended us to believe that what he wrote is true. To put things somewhat crudely, we might say that in a philosophical-type argument S intends to get A to believe that r by pointing out that certain propositions, which A already believes, are reasons for believing r. But S does not intend A to think that p and q are reasons for believing r because S intends A to believe this; rather, S expects that A will see that what S said is true by virtue of A's ability to reason from the premisses to the conclusion.

That there are such counter-examples to Grice's analysis is just what one should expect on the basis of certain *a priori* considerations. Grice's account of S-meaning is arrived at (in "Meaning") primarily by way of an abstraction from two types of cases: cases of "telling" someone that such-and-such is the case and cases of "telling" someone to do such-and-such. Thus, according to Grice, S meant that p by uttering x just in case S uttered x intending A to think that p on the basis (in part) of thinking that S intends A to think that p. It is implicit in Grice's account that S will intend A to take the fact that S intends A to think that p as evidence that S thinks that p (or, more commonly, thinks that he knows that p) and intend A to take the fact that S thinks (he knows) that p as evidence that p is the case. Suppose now that there are certain types of propositions such that it is well-known that, *ceteris paribus*, if p' is a proposition of this type, no one will take the fact that someone (no matter who) thinks he knows that p' as evidence that p' is the case. Since one cannot, in general, intend to bring about that which one knows one cannot bring about, it will follow from Grice's account of what it is for someone to mean that such-and-such is the case, that if p' is a proposition of this type, no one can mean that p'. But there is a large class of propositions for which ordinary empirical evidence (and so, *a fortiori*, the fact that a proposition of this type is believed by so-and-so) is irrelevant, at least in the sense that what is needed to believe that a proposition of this type is true is not new empirical evidence. This is true of most of the assertions made in journals of a theoretical or conceptual nature. For example, it is unlikely that anyone—ingratiating students apart—will believe that there are no analytical truths because he knows that Quine believes this to be true. So if Grice is right, no one could ever (or hardly ever) mean that p', where p' is a proposition of this type. But some people do say and mean that there are no analytical truths. So Grice is wrong. (We might express the objection being made by saying that Grice has overlooked the difference between sophists and cretans: if I put forward an argument intending to convince you that its conclusion is true, I cannot correctly be said to have *lied* to you, even though I know the conclusion is false and the argument invalid. To be a cretan I must intend you to think that p on my authority.)

This type of counter-example is not restricted to cases of S meaning that such-and-such is the case; it applies as well to cases of S meaning that A is to do such-and-such. For example, I could not *tell* you not to vote, but perhaps I could present you with a persuasive *practical* argument the conclusion of which is that you should not vote.

It is also relevant to note that a variation of the type of counter-example under discussion provides a counter-example to another claim of Grice's, viz., that if S utters x with the primary intention of producing in A the response r_1 by means of recognition of intention and also with the intention that the production in A of r_1 be sufficient for the production in A of some further response r_2, then S's intention to produce r_2 in A is no part of the characterization of what S meant by uttering x. In the cases considered in the preceding couple of paragraphs, S argues from premises already believed by A to an unknown conclusion. But there are also cases where S tells A that p and intends A's belief that p to be his reason for believing q (or doing ψ) and where S can nevertheless be said to have meant that q (or that A was to ψ). This might be the case were S to say, for example, "Don't swim in the water; it's shark infested", or "John's car broke down; so he won't be here".

(b) Counter-examples to the condition that S intend to produce r in A by means of recognition of intention are also provided by cases of *reminding* and *pointing out*.

    (i) A: "Now, what was that girl's name?"
        S: Holds up a rose; or, "Rose".
    (ii) A: "All Balliol men are brilliant."
        S: "Except Crumley-Gadswell."

In each of these cases S utters something x (utters 'Rose', or holds up a rose or utters 'Except Crumley-Gadswell') with the intention of thereby bringing it about that A is reminded that p; yet it need be no part of S's intention that the intended response be brought about by means of A's recognition of S's intention to produce that response; S knows that the mere utterance of x is enough to secure that A is reminded that p.

(iii) A: "A necessary condition of someone's meaning that p is that he utter a sentence which means "p"."

S: "But then one could never mean that p by uttering a sentence metaphorically."

Here S utters x with the intention of getting A to see, or of pointing out to A, that p (that such-and-such is a consequence of A's statement), but S does not, and indeed could not, intend to bring about this effect by means of recognition of intention. Still, we should want to say that S meant something.

In some of these cases S could be said to have the intention of producing in A the belief that p (e.g., where A had completely forgotten that p), but in other cases we should want to say that A already had (and was known by S to have) the latent belief that p, and in such cases it would be more accurate to say that S's intention was to produce in A the *activated* or *occurrent* belief that p. Thus, in all cases so far considered of S meaning that p, S utters x intending to bring it about that A has in mind the belief that p, although only in some cases does S actually intend to provide A with the belief that p. Another type of case which fits this description would be a case in which S utters, e.g., 'Rose earns 30 pounds a week, has her own car and a flat in London' with the intention of reviewing or "calling up" these facts about Rose known to both S and A with the intention of securing that A has all of the relevant facts about Rose in mind while deciding whether to marry her.

Analogous examples may be thought of where the intended response is a practical one. For example, after their marriage, Rose might remind or point out to A that he should be doing the washing-up. (Perhaps in some cases of this type we should say, as Grice has suggested, that S's intention is to restore A to activated intention.)[9]

I do not think that it can plausibly be denied that I have produced examples (i) in which S utters x with the primary intention of producing in A a certain response r and (ii) in which it is not

[9] "Utterer's Meaning and Intentions", p. 171.

the case that S intends part of A's reason for his response r to be based on A's recognition of S's intention to produce r in A and (iii) which would and should be classed as instances of S-meaning. This being so there seem to be only two lines of attack open to anyone who wishes to deny that I have produced genuine counter-examples to the condition requiring that the intended response be intended to be brought about by means of recognition of intention.

(1) In each example produced in this section S utters x intending to produce a certain response r in A but not intending to produce r in A by means of recognition of intention. It might be suggested that in one or more of the above types of cases there is some other response r' which S does intend to produce in A by means of recognition of intention and that it is in virtue of his uttering x with *this* intention that S means something by uttering x.

There may appear to be two candidate responses in the case where S argues that p from certain known premises. (i) It has been suggested that while, in this type of case, S does not intend to get A to believe that p by means of recognition of intention, S does intend A to think that S thinks p and does intend that at least part of A's reason for thinking that S thinks that p be that S intends A to think that S thinks that p. Perhaps, the suggestion goes, S means that p in virtue of his intention to produce in A, by means of recognition of intention, the belief that S thinks that p. (ii) When S presents an argument to convince A that p he certainly does not intend A to accept the argument on the basis of S's accepting it, but he may intend A's reason for *entertaining* the argument to be that S wants him to. So perhaps in this type of case S means something in virtue of his intention to get A to follow the argument, think of possible objections, etc.

It is even more difficult to find a candidate response in the re-minding and pointing out cases, but here, too, it has been suggested that S intends A to think that S thinks that p and intends A's thinking that S thinks that p to be based partly on A's recognition of S's intention to get A to think that S thinks that p.

We have, then, the merits of the following two suggestions to consider. (i) In the "argument" or "reminding" or "pointing out" cases S means that p by uttering x only if S intends to produce in A the belief that S thinks that p and intends at least part of A's reason for thinking that S thinks that p to be that S

intends A to think that S thinks that p. (ii) In the "argument" cases S means that p by uttering x only if S intends A to entertain a certain argument the conclusion of which is that p and intends at least part of A's reason for entertaining the argument to be that S intends A to entertain the argument.

I have two replies to these suggestions. First, even if these suggestions were true, this line of defence would constitute a significant retreat from Grice's original account. Any account of what it is for someone to mean something by uttering x must be inextricably tied to an account of *what* is meant by uttering x. Now it was essential to Grice's original theory that S meant that such-and-such was the case by uttering x just in case S uttered x intending to produce in A, by means of recognition of intention, the belief that such-and-such was the case. Thus, the above examples constitute at least counter-examples to Grice's account of what it is for someone to mean that such-and-such is the case, and, consequently, to adopt either of the above suggestions would amount to the adoption of a quite different theory. (This same objection can be made, *mutatis mutandis*, with regard to similar suggestions for an account of what it is for someone to mean that someone is to do such-and-such.) Secondly, both suggestions are palpably false. That (i) is false at least with regard to the "argument" cases may be seen by noting that in many instances where S argues that p it is already mutual knowledge* between S and A that S believes that p. For example, we both may know that I firmly and sincerely believe that this is the best of all possible worlds; my purpose in arguing that this is the best of all possible worlds is to convince *you* that it is. That (i) is false with regard to the "reminding" and "pointing out" cases may be seen by noting that in most cases in which S succeeds in reminding or pointing out to A that p he will also succeed in reminding or pointing out to A that S thinks that p. Suggestion (ii), on the other hand, would be most unattractive even if an intention to secure that A "entertains" a certain argument (or proposition?) were a constant feature of the type of case it is meant to accommodate; for it is clear that such an intention would only apply to a limited range of cases of S meaning that such-and-such is the case, and so taking this way out would commit one to saying that the conditions necessary for S meaning that such-and-such is the case vary from one type of case to the other. Moreover, since the "argument" and "pointing out" cases overlap, it would seem to be false that whenever one argues that p from certain premisses one intends one's audience to "entertain" the argument put forward.

(2) A different line of attack would be to argue that the purported counter-examples are "derivative" from or "parasitic" upon cases of "telling" and are therefore to be explained in terms of and as departures from this "primary" case of *S*-meaning. I agree that there are cases which one should not count as counter-examples to Grice's account of *S*-meaning, even though in such cases *S* does not intend to produce a response in *A* by means of recognition of intention and even though one would be naturally inclined to say of such cases that *S* meant something. For example, one might say to a counter-suggestible child, "Do keep banging on your drum!" with the intention of getting him to *cease* banging on the drum. Here, I think, one would be inclined to say that one told the child to keep banging on the drum, and yet there is no response which one intends to bring about by means of recognition of intention: one intends the child to cease banging because he thinks one intends him to keep banging. I should think it wrong to consider this type of case a *counter-example* to Grice's theory; for it would seem that we are inclined to say that the speaker "told" the child to persist in banging the drum in virtue of his *pretending to tell* him this in the primary sense of the word 'tell'. But what kind of explanation could be given to show that the above examples are dependent upon cases of "telling" for their status as instances of *S*-meaning?

III

AN ACCOUNT OF S-MEANING

Introduction

WHAT is it for someone to mean something by (or in) uttering x? We began seeking an answer to this question by considering what seemed to be the most plausible account to date, that put forward by Grice. On Grice's view, to mean something by uttering x is just to utter x intending to produce in some person a certain type of response in a certain type of way. The only restraint on the type of response is that it must be something which is within the control of the audience, at least in the sense that it is the type of response for which the audience may have reasons. The only restraint on the way in which the response is to be produced by uttering x is that S must intend that at least part of A's reason for his response r will be that S uttered x intending to produce response r in A. One knows what S meant if, and only if, one knows what response S intended to produce in A.

I want to retain the condition that S meant something by uttering x only if S uttered x intending to produce some response in A. On the assumption that this condition is necessary and on the assumption that the mutual knowledge* conditions adequately deal with the problems they were meant to deal with, this leaves at least two main problems to be solved before we shall have arrived at an adequate and correct account of S-meaning.

One problem, which has to do with the specification of what S meant, was noticed in section I. 3, where it was remarked that even if correct, Grice's suggestion that what is meant is determined by, and only by, the value of 'r' does not provide a criterion for determining what S meant, but only a criterion for determining what must be determined if one is to determine what S meant. No account of S-meaning will be complete unless it provides a definite means for specifying what S meant by uttering x.

A more fundamental problem arises out of the fact that the restraint placed by Grice on the way in which S must intend to produce the relevant response r in A is much too restrictive, leaving out all but one type of instance of S-meaning. So we want to find a new way of completing the sentence form 'S meant something by uttering x only if S uttered x intending to produce in A a certain response r by means . . .'.

My procedure in this chapter is, first, to provide a definiens for each of the sentence forms 'by uttering x S meant that such-and-such was the case' and 'by uttering x S meant that A was to do such-and-such' (the bulk of this is done in sections III. 1 and III. 2). In section III. 5, I argue that S meant something by (or in) uttering x if and only if by (or in) uttering x S meant that such-and-such was the case or I, for some A, S meant that A was to do such-and-such. This is my solution to the first of the above-mentioned problems. Roughly, essentially, and apart from mutual knowledge* conditions, I argue that S meant that such-and-such was the case if and only if S uttered x intending to cause in A the activated belief that such-and-such was the case and intending his utterance x to cause A to have the activated belief that such-and-such was the case at least partly by virtue of A's recognition (belief) that x is related in a certain way R to (the type of response) thinking that such-and-such was the case. In the definiens for 'by uttering x S meant that A was to do such-and-such' the intended response is A's doing such-and-such; otherwise the two definitions are essentially identical. Hence, my solution to the second of the above-mentioned problems is that S meant something by uttering x only if S uttered x intending to produce in A a certain response r by means of A's recognition that x is related in a certain way R to the type of response to which r belongs.

It will be convenient if, at the outset, the expressions 'S meant that such-and-such was the case' and 'S meant that A was to do such-and-such' are replaced, respectively, by the expressions 'S meant that p' and 'S meant that A was to ψ'. The only allowable substituends for 'p' will be expressions which could complete the sentence form 'John believes that . . .'; the only allowable substituends for 'ψ' will be expressions which could complete sentences of the form 'John will . . .' or 'John intends to . . .'.

III.1 *S meant that p*

The examples so far considered in which S means that p divide up, broadly speaking, into two types of cases. On the one hand we have cases of *S* "telling" *A* that *p*, where *S* utters *x* intending to produce in *A* the belief that *p* by means of *A*'s recognition of this intention, and, on the other hand, we have cases of reminding, pointing out, arguing from known premisses to an unknown conclusion, etc., where *S* utters *x* intending to produce in *A* the belief that *p* or the *activated* belief that *p* (i.e., intends *A* to have in mind the belief that *p*), but not intending to produce this response by means of recognition of intention. There is at least one thing all of these cases have in common, viz. : in each case *S* utters *x* intending thereby to cause in *A* the *activated* belief that *p*.

I propose to accept provisionally the condition, inherited in part from Grice, that *S* meant that *p* by uttering *x* only if *S* uttered *x* intending thereby to cause in *A* the activated belief that *p*. Its acceptance will cease to be provisional when, in sections III.3 and III.4, the alleged objections to this condition are dealt with.

Needless to say, this condition is not a sufficient condition for *S* meaning that *p*, if for no other reason than that it is met by each counter-example described in section II.1. But there still remains the question whether the mutual knowledge* conditions are merely required for *S* to be *telling* *A* that *p* or whether these conditions are required for all instances of *S* meaning that *p*. That the latter is the case is strongly suggested by what follows. We know that at least some instances of *S* uttering *x* with the intention of reminding *A* that *p* are instances of *S* meaning that *p* by uttering *x*. Now suppose it were claimed that a sufficient condition of *S* having meant that *p* by uttering *x* is that *S* uttered *x* intending to remind *A* that *p*. Each of the following examples would be a counter-example to that claim.

(i) *S* knows that *A* is trying to remember so-and-so's name. *S*, unbeknown to *A*, places a bowl of roses in *A*'s room, intending that *A* should see the roses and be reminded that so-and-so's name is Rose. *A* is intended to think that the roses were placed in his room purely for decorative reasons.

(ii) Again *S* places a bowl of roses in *A*'s room with the intention of reminding *A* that so-and-so's name is Rose. This time, however, *S* intends *A* to recognize that *S* placed the roses in *A*'s room intending to remind *A* that so-and-so's name is Rose, but also intending *A* to *think* that *S* intends *A* to think that *S* placed the roses in the room purely for decorative reasons.

(iii) Again *S* intends the roses to remind *A* that so-and-so's name is Rose, only this time *S* intends *A* to reason: "*S* intends me to think that he intends me to think that he put the roses in my room purely for decorative reasons, but I recognize that he really intends me to recognize that his intention in putting the roses in my room was to remind me that so-and-so's name is Rose."

In none of these examples is it the case that *S* meant that so-and-so's name was Rose. Clearly, similar examples may be constructed where *S* intends to point out to *A* that *p* or to convince *A* that *p* on the basis of *A*'s prior acceptance of certain premisses, or, for that matter, any type of case in which *S* utters *x* intending to produce in *A* the belief or activated belief that *p*. Let us begin, then, with the following set of necessary conditions.

(A) *S* meant that *p* by (or in) uttering *x* *only if S* uttered *x* intending thereby to realize a certain state of affairs *E* which is (intended by *S* to be) such that the obtainment of *E* is sufficient for *S* and a certain audience *A* mutually knowing* (or believing*) that *E* obtains and that *E* is conclusive (very good or good) evidence that *S* uttered *x* intending

(1) to cause in *A* the activated belief that *p*;
(2) to realize *E*.

The next example shows that the conditions of (A) are not jointly sufficient for *S* meaning that *p*.

S, a rather advanced neuro-physiologist, knows that by striking a certain chord on a piano he will emit a sound of a certain frequency which will set off a certain neuro-physiological process in the brain of any person of a certain type which will result in that person's remembering what word he first learned as a child. *A*, let us suppose, is *S*'s assistant; so the above—along with the fact that *A* is a person of the relevant type and the fact that *S* knows on independent grounds what word *A* first learned —is mutual knowledge* between *S* and *A*. Finally, suppose that *S* strikes the relevant chord intending to cause *A* to remember that '*Gesundheit*' was the first word *A* learned and intending the satisfaction of the mutual knowledge* conditions.

I do not believe that it would be correct to say that by striking the chord *S* meant that '*Gesundheit*' was the first word *A* learned. In order to see what precludes the neuro-physiologist from having meant that '*Gesundheit*' was the first word *A* learned it will be helpful to contrast the preceding example with the following two examples.

(i) *A* is trying to remember what musical instrument Liberace plays. *S* strikes a piano chord with the intention of reminding *A* that Liberace plays the piano.

(ii) This is the same as (i), only instead of striking a piano chord *S* utters the sentence 'Liberace plays the piano'.

I believe that with regard to examples (i) and (ii) one is inclined to say that *S* meant that Liberace plays the piano: in (i) *S* meant this by (or in) striking the piano chord and in (ii) *S* meant this by (or in) uttering 'Liberace plays the piano'. What precludes *S* from having meant that *p* in the 'neuro-physiologist' example is, I believe, the way in which striking the piano chord is intended to cause *A* to remember that *p*. Specifically, the relevant difference between the "neuro-physiologist" example and the first "Liberace" example seems to be this. In both examples striking the chord is intended to cause *A* to remember that *p* but in the "Liberace" example, unlike the "neuro-physiologist" example, striking the piano chord is intended to cause *A* to remember that *p* as a result of (or by virtue of) *A* recognizing that there is a certain relation (association, connection, or correlation) between *S*'s striking the chord and the belief that *p* (i.e., the belief that Liberace plays the piano). This is also the relevant difference between the "neuro-physiologist" example and the second "Liberace" example: in (ii) *S* intends his utterance of 'Liberace plays the piano' to cause *A* to remember that Liberace plays the piano by virtue of *A*'s recognition that 'Liberace plays the piano' is a conventional means for making known one's intention to produce in an audience the belief (or activated belief) that Liberace plays the piano. Thus, the relevant difference between (i) and (ii) is that in (i) *S* intends his utterance *x* to be a cause of *A*'s believing *p* by virtue of *A*'s awareness of a certain "natural" association or relation between *x* and (the response-type) believing *p* and in (ii) *S* intends his utterance *x* to be causally efficacious by virtue of *A*'s awareness that *x* is conventionally correlated with the belief that *p* (or, to quiet Quinean qualms, correlated with (the response-type) believing *p*).

So it seems reasonable to think that an instance of *S* uttering *x* with the intention of thereby reminding *A* that *p* is an instance of *S* meaning that *p* by uttering *x* only if *S* utters *x* intending to cause in A the activated belief that p and intending that his utterance x be a cause of A's having the activated belief that p at least partly by virtue of A's recognition (belief) that x is related in a certain way R to the belief that p (or, what for me will be the same, (the response-type) believing (thinking) that p). And if this is reasonable, then it will be reasonable to think that S meant that p by uttering x only if S uttered x intending to cause in A the activated belief that p and intending that his utterance x be a cause of A's having the activated belief that p at least partly by virtue of A's recognition (belief) that x is related in a certain way R to the belief that p. For the same type of considerations as those which apply to cases of "reminding" apply as well to the "pointing out", "calling up" ("fact review"), and "argument" cases; and in cases of "telling" A that p it is clear that there is at least one relation between x and the belief that p which S must intend A to recognize if S is to succeed in producing in A the belief that p, viz., that S uttered x intending to produce in A the belief that p. The conditions of (A) may therefore be replaced by those of (B).

> (B) S meant that p by (or in) uttering x *only if S* uttered x intending thereby to realize a certain state of affairs E which is (intended by S to be) such that the obtainment of E is sufficient for S and a certain audience A mutually knowing* (or believing*) that E obtains and that E is conclusive (very good or good) evidence that S uttered x intending
>
> (1) to cause in A the activated belief that p;
> (2) satisfaction of (1) to be achieved, at least in part, by virtue of A's belief that x is related in a certain way R to the belief that p;
> (3) to realize E.

In Chapter I we saw the need, in restating Grice's definition, to make explicit the condition that S intend A to think that S intends to produce a certain response r in A *on the basis of thinking* that S uttered x. Since an object or event will be evidence that such-and-such is the case only *qua* being an object or event of a certain *sort*, the restatement of Grice's account made explicit reference to a special "feature(s) f". Subsequently this explicit reference was submerged when the mutual knowledge* conditions were added, but only submerged and not erased: S's utterance x

will be the key constituent of the state of affairs E and it will have this role in virtue of having certain of its features and not in virtue of other of its features. There are now two further points to be made apropos of the most recently added demand that S intend a certain relation to obtain between x and the intended response. (1) The fact that x is f will not serve as a means for making known to A the particular response S intends to produce in A unless the fact that x is f relates (or is thought by A to relate) x in a certain way to the type of response to which r belongs. (2) If, as claimed, condition (2) of (B) is a necessary condition of S meaning that p, then A will not take the fact that S uttered x as evidence that S meant thereby that p unless A thinks that x is related in way R to the belief that p. So the requirement that S intend x to be (thought by A to be) related in a certain way R to the belief that p will have, as it were, a double life: if S meant that p by uttering x and if S succeeded in satisfying the intentions with which he uttered x, then x will have been (thought by A to be) related in a certain way R to the belief that p and at least partly in virtue of this fact S's utterance x will have been both a cause of A's having the activated belief that p and evidence that S uttered x intending to produce in A the activated belief that p.

(B) still does not keep out quite as much as one might wish.

(1) There are cases where, by uttering x, S both means something and intends to cause A to believe that p, but where S does not mean that p. For example, we may not wish to say that in prescribing to A that he ought to believe that his wife was faithful, S meant that A's wife was faithful, a proposition S may not wish to commit himself to. And, I suppose, in suitable circumstances one person might even command another person to believe, or to make it the case that he believes, that a certain proposition is true. (B) would commit us to saying that the person would mean that that proposition is true. (These examples are also counter-examples to the alleged sufficiency of Grice's analysans. This is one of the objections alluded to in Chapter II, p. 42.)

(2) Imagine a person who suffers from the complaint that whenever anyone utters the sound 'Urf!' he immediately becomes obsessed with the wholly irrational belief that his dog Rover is about to be run over. Now suppose that S takes delight in putting

poor *A* in this horrible state by uttering 'Urf!'. Even if all of the conditions of (B) are satisfied, I still think it would be incorrect to say that by uttering 'Urf!' *S* meant that Rover was about to be run over.

(3) (B) also commits us to saying that in presenting Salome with the head of St. John the Baptist on a charger, Herod meant that St. John the Baptist was dead.

Let us begin with (3). What are we to say about examples of this type? Well, one thing that might be said is that in presenting Salome with the head of St. John the Baptist, Herod meant that St. John the Baptist was dead. This does not strike me as a wildly implausible thing to say. Consider an analogous case.

> (3a) A: "Let's play squash."
>   S: Holds up his bandaged leg.

Here, I think, one would say, intuitively, that by holding up his leg *S* meant that he could not play, or that he could not play because his leg was injured; yet it would seem that the only difference between (3) and (3a) which is possibly relevant is that the "inference" *A* has to make in the "bandaged leg" example is slightly less direct than in the case of St. John the Baptist's head, although in both cases one could make the relevant inference without any assistance on the part of *S*.

Grice has objected that while we may say that (in (3a)) *S* meant that he could not play squash by holding up his bandaged leg, he could *not* mean thereby that his leg was bandaged.[1] But, in the first place, even this is not an objection to the point I am trying to make, which is that there is no relevant difference between (3) and (3a), so that if we may say that *S* meant that he could not play squash, then—by parity of reason—we may say that Herod meant that St. John the Baptist was dead (it was not suggested that Herod meant that there was a severed head on his charger). In the second place, I think that it is false that *S* could not mean that his leg was bandaged by holding up his bandaged leg. Consider (3b).

> (3b) A: "I've heard that your leg is bandaged. Is it true?"
>   S: Holds up his bandaged leg.

Here, I think, one would say that *S* meant that his leg was bandaged.

---

[1] "Utterer's Meaning and Intentions", p. 170.

However, if it should turn out to be desirable to eliminate examples of type (3), this would not be difficult to do. This can be done by specifying that the relation R between S's utterance x and the belief that p which A is intended to recognize must not be such that S's utterance x will provide A with *evidence* that p without the mediation of an intention on the part of S to produce in A, by uttering x, the belief that p. And if the reader finds it implausible to allow that Herod meant that St. John the Baptist was dead, he may treat the proposed way in which cases of this type may be excluded from the definition as an optional condition which he may add to the analysans should his intuitions so compel him. I shall not.

A few general remarks will place us in a position to deal with cases of types (1) and (2). If S meant that p by uttering x, then not only will S have intended to produce in A the belief (or activated belief) that p, S will also have intended that A have *reasons* for his belief that p (although only in some cases does S intend to *supply* A with reasons for believing that p). Now it is almost always the case that if one holds ρ as a reason for believing that p, one will think that ρ provides, in some sense, grounds for thinking that p is true. Let us call reasons which are held in this way "truth-supporting" reasons. One's reasons for believing p *need not* be truth-supporting; one might have moral or prudential grounds for thinking that p. This distinction gives us a means for eliminating counter-examples of type (1); for we may say that a necessary condition for S meaning that p by uttering x is that S intend A to have truth-supporting reasons for his belief that p. And the requirement that S intend A to have reasons for thinking that p will also serve to eliminate counter-examples of type (2).

It will be convenient at this point to introduce the following notational device. Let

'S intends to produce in A the response r/ρ' = df.

'S intends to produce in A the response r for which he intends A to have the reason(s) ρ.'

If A is intended to have truth-supporting reasons for his response (i.e., his belief), then this will be marked by writing

'$\rho(t)$'.

It may then be said that S means that p by uttering x only if

S intends that there be some ρ such that his utterance of *x* causes *A* to have the activated belief that $p/\rho(t)$.

The intuitive justification for this condition is at least twofold. First, it captures the demand that meaning and communication be *rational* in a certain way; secondly, it reflects the fact that communication, in general, aims at the production of knowledge and not merely belief. Consequently it may seem that a more intuitive formulation of the needed condition would be both possible and desirable. However, I feel that the above formulation of the needed condition will prove most useful in the end, partly because of two forthcoming considerations. One is that we shall find that a similar restriction is required in the definiens for 'by uttering *x* *S* meant that *A* was to ψ'; the other is that, in the general account of speech acts to be offered in Chapter IV, an essential ingredient in the determination of the "illocutionary force" of an utterance is the reason or reasons *S* intends *A* to have for the primary response *S* intends to produce in *A*, and so it is desirable to have a formulation which brings this feature explicitly into view.

Definition (B) may be revised accordingly to give us (C).

> (C) *S* meant that *p* by (or in) uttering *x* *only if* *S* uttered *x* intending thereby to realize a certain state of affairs *E* which is (intended by *S* to be) such that the obtainment of *E* is sufficient for *S* and a certain audience *A* mutually knowing* (or believing*) that *E* obtains and that *E* is conclusive (very good or good) evidence that *S* uttered *x* intending
>
> (1) there to be some ρ such that *S*'s utterance of *x* causes in *A* the activated belief that $p/\rho(t)$;
> (2) satisfaction of (1) to be achieved, at least in part, by virtue of *A*'s belief that *x* is related in a certain way *R* to the belief that *p*;
> (3) to realize *E*.

III.2 *S meant that p and S meant that A was to ψ*

The account of what it is for someone to mean that *p* so far arrived at requires at least one further minor adjustment before sufficiency may be claimed for its conditions; but before any further adjustments are made it will be well to offer the following parallel account, also not quite sufficient, of what it is for someone to mean that A is to ψ.

S meant that A was to ψ by (or in) uttering x *only if* S uttered x intending thereby to realize a certain state of affairs E which is (intended by S to be) such that the obtainment of E is sufficient for S and A mutually knowing* (or believing*) that E obtains and that E is conclusive (very good or good) evidence that S uttered x intending

(1) there to be some ρ such that S's utterance of x causes A to ψ/ρ;
(2) satisfaction of (1) to be achieved, at least in part, by virtue of A's belief that x is related in a certain way R to (the act-type) ψ-ing;
(3) to realize E.

There are a few features of this set of conditions which call for special comment.

(1) The demand that S intend A to have a reason for ψ-ing is the demand that the intended act be rational, and it is needed to rule out the same type of case as its counterpart in the definition of 'S meant that p'. Thus one might imagine a man so neurotically terrified of cats that whenever he hears the sound 'meow' he begins running around in circles—he just can't help himself. Condition (1) above precludes us from having to say that by uttering 'meow' S meant that A was to run around in circles.

(2) The conditions for S meaning that p allow that S may mean that p by uttering x even though S intends his utterance x to provide A with reason(s) for thinking that p without the mediation of S's intentions (e.g. the "Herod" example). Analogously, the conditions for S meaning that A is to ψ allow that S may mean that A is to ψ by uttering x even though S intends his utterance x to provide A with a reason for ψ-ing without the mediation of S's intentions. Thus, by posting a vicious dog at the entrance to his home, S may have meant that A was to stay away. Once again, my intuitions do not balk at this result, and once again there is an easy way of eliminating such cases should it be desirable to do so: it may be done by specifying that the relation R between S's utterance x and (the act-type) ψ-ing which A is intended to recognize must not be such that S's utterance

x will provide A with a reason for ψ-ing without the mediation of an intention on the part of S to cause A to ψ.

(3) A disanalogy between the definitions of 'S meant that p' and 'S meant that A was to ψ' is that in the former but not the latter the intended response is an activated propositional attitude. Grice has suggested achieving symmetry by replacing A's ψ-ing with *an (activated) intention on the part of A to ψ* as the intended response in the account of imperative utterances.[2] But while this would perhaps add a certain attractiveness to the account of S-meaning, it would also, I fear, open the way for certain counter-examples in which S intends to produce in A the intention to ψ but does not (and is known by A not to) intend A actually to ψ.

(4) Finally, a word about the definiendum, 'S meant that A was to ψ'. In ordinary discourse, to say that S meant that A was to ψ often implies something fairly strong, e.g. that S was ordering A to ψ. If I politely request you to pass the salt, it may be misleading to say that I meant that you were to pass me the salt. There is, I suppose, a certain amount of regimentation being imposed in our choice of a definiendum, but it should be noted that it is compatible with the account of what it is for someone to mean that A is to ψ that the value of 'ψ' may be, say, passing the salt *if one pleases*.

As I remarked earlier, there is a further minor revision to be made before sufficiency may be claimed for the conditions of either definition. The importance of the adjustment to be made lies mainly in certain of its consequences, not all of which will be explored in this chapter.

Consider the most recent analysans for the account of what it is for S to mean that p by uttering x, i.e. (C) on p. 58. The problem is this. If the conditions of (C) were jointly sufficient for S meaning that p by uttering x and if S uttered x with the intentions specified in (C), then not only will S have meant thereby that p, he will also have meant by uttering x that he uttered x intending to cause in A the activated belief that p, that he intends A to have reasons for his belief that p, that he intends his utterance x to cause in A the activated belief that p at least partly by virtue of A's recognition that x is related in a certain way R to the belief that p, and so on for all the other beliefs which (C) requires S to intend, in uttering x, to produce in A in addition to the belief (or activated belief) that p. But

[2] "Utterer's Meaning and Intentions", p. 166.

if S means, say, that the cat is on the mat by uttering 'The cat is on the mat', it will not be the case that in uttering 'The cat is on the mat' S will also have meant that he uttered 'The cat is on the mat' intending to produce in A the belief that the cat was on the mat. So the conditions of (C) are not jointly sufficient for S meaning that p by uttering x. The same type of objection can be made against the above account of what it is for S to mean that A is to ψ.

To see that the definitions have this consequence, suppose that S utters x with the intentions specified in (C). S will, in that event, intend to produce a certain state of affairs E which is mutually known* by S and A to be evidence that S uttered x intending to produce in A the belief (or activated belief) that p. Hence, S intends by uttering x to cause in A the belief that S uttered x intending to cause in A the activated belief that p, and since S intends his utterance x to be *evidence* that S uttered x intending to cause in A the activated belief that p, S intends his utterance x to be a cause of A's having the belief that S uttered x intending to cause in A the activated belief that p by virtue of A's recognition that x is related in a certain way to the belief that S uttered x intending to cause in A the activated belief that p. And since all of this is made known by the state of affairs E (viz., the fact that S uttered x in the circumstances), it follows that if (C) provided sufficient conditions, S will have meant by uttering x that he uttered x intending to cause in A the activated belief that p. Clearly, this is unacceptable.

It is worth noticing that Grice's account of S-meaning is open to the same type of objection. Suppose S utters x intending to inform A that p by means of recognition of this intention. In order to inform A that p, S will, in uttering x, intend to produce in A the belief that S believes that he knows that p; but S will intend A's reason for thinking that S thinks that he knows that p to be, at least in part, the fact that S uttered x intending A to think that S thinks he knows that p. So it is a *de facto* consequence of Grice's account that whenever S utters x intending to produce a certain response r in A by means of recognition of intention, there will always be certain beliefs, other than the primary response aimed at, which S also intends to produce in A by means of recognition of intention. So it follows from Grice's account that whenever S means something he will mean a lot more than he bargained for. This is the second respect alluded to in section II.2, p. 42, in which Grice's analysans is not sufficient.

What we want to say is that if *S* means that *p* by uttering *x*, then, while he must intend to produce in *A* certain beliefs in addition to the belief (or activated belief) that *p*, these other intentions to produce beliefs do not constitute separate acts of meaning; rather they are necessary constituents of *S*'s act of meaning that *p*, or a necessary part of the characterization of *S*'s act of meaning that *p*. The problem is to find the relevant difference between *S*'s intention to produce in *A* the belief that *p* and, say, his intention to produce in *A* the belief that *S* intends to produce in *A* the belief that *p*. In other words: what is the relevant difference between, say, *S*'s intention to produce in *A* the belief that *p* and his intention to produce in *A* the belief that he intends to produce in *A* the belief that *p* such that in virtue of this difference *S* means that *p* by uttering *x* but does not mean by uttering *x* that he intends to produce in *A* the belief that *p*?

One relevant difference which comes quickly to mind (a difference of which I have been tacitly availing myself all along) is that when it is true to say that *S* meant that *p* by uttering *x*, then *S*'s intention to produce in *A* the activated belief that *p* is the *primary* intention with which *S* uttered *x*, whereas *S*'s intention to produce in *A* the belief that *S* uttered *x* intending to produce in *A* the activated belief that *p* is merely a *secondary* intention *S* had in uttering *x*—one carried on the back of the primary intention—an intention *S* had in uttering *x* as a result of having the primary intention to produce in *A* the activated belief that *p*.

Generally, when a person does an act *X* a distinction can be made between: (i) the intention(s) *with which* that person did *X*, and (ii) certain other intentions that person merely had *in* doing *X*. If an intention *i* is an intention with which one did *X*, then *i* will be an intention one had in doing *X*, but the converse need not hold. To specify one's primary intention in doing *X*—the intention with which one did *X*—is to give one's reason for doing *X*. This does not apply to all of the intentions one had in doing *X*.

I believe that this asymmetry applies to the difference between *S*'s intention to produce in *A* the belief (or activated belief) that *p* and the other beliefs *S* must intend to produce in *A* when he means that *p* (or that *A* is to *ψ*), and I believe it is this asymmetry which accounts for why, in uttering *x*, *S* meant that *p* and not, say, that he uttered *x* intending to produce in *A* the belief that *p*. (*S* may, of course, utter *x* with more than one primary intention, and in such cases he may mean more than one thing; in some cases it may not be clear what *S*'s primary intention was, and to the extent that this is so it will not be clear what *S* meant.) Finally, I submit the following two definitions.

S meant that *p* by (or in) uttering *x* iff *S* uttered *x* intending thereby to realize a certain state of affairs *E* which is (intended by *S* to be) such that the obtainment of *E* is sufficient for *S* and a certain audience *A* mutually knowing* (or believing*) that *E* obtains and that *E* is conclusive (very good or good) evidence that *S* uttered *x* with the primary intention

(1) that there be some ρ such that *S*'s utterance of *x* causes in *A* the activated belief that $p/\rho(t)$;

and intending

(2) satisfaction of (1) to be achieved, at least in part, by virtue of *A*'s belief that *x* is related in a certain way *R* to the belief that *p*;

(3) to realize *E*.

S meant that *A* was to ψ by (or in) uttering *x* iff *S* uttered *x* intending thereby to realize a certain state of affairs *E* which is (intended by *S* to be) such that the obtainment of *E* is sufficient for *S* and *A* mutually knowing* (or believing*) that *E* obtains and that *E* is conclusive (very good or good) evidence that *S* uttered *x* with the primary intention

(1) that there be some ρ such that *S*'s utterance of *x* causes *A* to ψ/ρ;

and intending

(2) satisfaction of (1) to be achieved, at least in part, by virtue of *A*'s belief that *x* is related in a certain way *R* to (the act-type) ψ-ing;

(3) to realize *E*.

The mutual knowledge* conditions will have to be adjusted slightly to accommodate certain utterances in the absence of an audience (this is done in section III.4), but, for all practical purposes, these definitions may be regarded as final, which is not, however, to say that they will encounter no further problems.

In fact, one such problem will now be raised and I hope that its solution will serve to confirm at least certain features of our definitions.

A consequence of the latest revision is that if S utters x with just those intentions specified in either definition, then he *cannot* mean by uttering x that his primary intention in uttering x is to produce in A the belief that p (or to get A to ψ). In view of the preceding, this may hardly seem objectionable. But suppose that S uttered x with just those intentions specified in the account of what it is for S to mean that p and suppose that what S uttered (the value of 'x') was

σ_1: My primary intention in uttering this sentence is to produce in you—by means of recognition of intention—the belief that p.

While it may not seem objectionable to say that in uttering σ_1, S meant that p, it does *seem* objectionable to say that S did not also mean just what he said, viz., that his primary intention was . . . After all, we know what σ_1 means and we seem to understand what S would mean by uttering it; indeed, unless S is lying it would seem that what he said is true. But if S uttered σ_1 with just those intentions specified in the definiens for 'S meant that p' and if by uttering σ_1 S meant that his primary intention was . . ., then we have a counter-example to the above definitions, a counter-example, as we will shortly see, with quite serious consequences for the entire programme we are engaged in.

It is essential to the programme of providing an account of the meaning of utterance-types in terms of a basic account of S-meaning that what S means by uttering x is not at all determined by what is uttered, i.e. by the value of 'x'. As I remarked in section I.3, this does not mean that one can do or say whatever one likes and mean thereby anything one pleases to mean: one must utter x with the relevant intentions, and not any value of 'x' will be appropriate to this end. But whatever the value of 'x' is, it is essential to our account of meaning that if one can reasonably expect to utter x with those intentions purported to be necessary and sufficient for meaning that p, then one will mean thereby that p, no matter what x is. Another way of making this point is this. If the only difference between two utterances is that in one case S utters x and in the other S utters y, then what S means by uttering x is identical with what

S means by uttering *y*. The importance of this condition is that if it were the case that what *S* meant by uttering *x* were determined, even in part, by the meaning of *x*, then this would, on the face of it, render circular an account of what *x* means in terms of what is or would be meant by uttering *x*. And the serious problem with the objection raised is that, if true, it would show that what is meant by uttering *x* at least sometimes is determined by the meaning of *x*.

For suppose that instead of uttering σ_1, *S* had simply uttered

σ_2: *p* [e.g. 'The cat is on the mat.']

And let us suppose that the only difference between the two utterances is in what *S* uttered. For instance, we might imagine that *S* desired to inform *A*, by means of recognition of intention, that the cat was on the mat. He therefore had to utter *something* which would make known to *A* his intentions. In the one case he utters 'My primary intention in uttering this sentence is to inform you—by means of recognition of intention—that the cat is on the mat' (σ_1), and in the other case he simply utters 'The cat is on the mat' (σ_2); but the only difference between the two cases is in the means used to make known his intentions, i.e. in the value of '*x*'. The problem, of course, is that while the only difference between the two acts is what is uttered, it does not *seem* plausible to say that what *S* meant by uttering σ_1 was identical with what *S* meant by uttering σ_2.

So we are faced with the following complex dilemma. If by uttering σ_1 *S* meant that his primary intention . . ., and if *S* uttered σ_1 with just those intentions purported to be necessary and sufficient for his meaning that *p*, then not all of the conditions of the account of what it is for *S* to mean that *p* are necessary, for the analysans will then exclude at least one case of *S* meaning that *p*. Even worse, if in uttering σ_1 *S* meant that his primary intention . . . and if in uttering σ_2 *S* did not mean that his primary intention . . . and if the only difference between these two cases is in the means used to make known *S*'s intentions, then we have at least one case where what is meant is determined by the meaning of the sentence *S* uttered, and this would seem to call into question the whole enterprise we are engaged in.

One way out would be to deny, *a priori*, that *S* can utter σ_1 with just those intentions specified in the definition. This line might be taken in either of two ways. (1) It may seem that the relevant difference between σ_1 and σ_2 is that were S to utter σ_1 his intention would be to produce in A, by means of recognition of intention, the belief that S uttered σ_1 intending to produce in A, by means of recognition of intention, the belief that p, whereas if S were to utter σ_2 his intention would merely be to produce in A, by means of recognition of intention, the belief that p. But we have already seen that this way out is unavailable, since S cannot intend to produce in A the belief that p by means of recognition of intention without, in effect, intending to produce in A—by means of recognition of intention—the belief that S uttered x intending to produce in A the belief that p by means of recognition of intention. (2) It may be argued that σ_1 does not present a counter-example, because one who uttered σ_1 would have *two* primary intentions: one to produce in A the belief that p, the other to produce in A the belief that a primary intention in uttering σ_1 was to produce in A the belief that p. However, this way out may easily be side-stepped by using as our example the sentence 'My *only* primary intention in uttering this is . . .' It seems incredible to think that S could not utter a sentence which "explicitly describes" those and only those intentions S had in uttering that sentence.

Alternatively, one may deny, as I propose to do, that in uttering σ_1 S does in fact mean that his primary intention is to produce in A the belief that p (etc.). Taking this line does not (as noticed in Chapter I) preclude one from saying that by 'My primary intention . . .' S meant "My primary intention . . ."

Suppose that there can be found a sentence σ_3, such that (i) σ_3 means the same as σ_1, but (ii) it is quite clear that one would want to say that S would *not* mean by uttering σ_3 that his primary intention was to produce in A the belief that p (etc.). If such a sentence could be found, this would give us extremely good grounds for denying that by uttering 'My primary intention in uttering this is . . .' (σ_1) S meant that his primary intention . . .; for it seems highly reasonable to assume that if two sentences have the same meaning, then what would be meant by "subscriptively" uttering the one would also be meant by "subscriptively" uttering the other.

Consider now the explicit performative

σ_3: I (hereby) tell you that p.

(i) Presumably, as Austin so forcefully urged, in uttering σ_3 one would not mean *that* one was telling *A* that *p*; one who utters 'I hereby tell you that *p*' is not saying *that* he is performing the speech act of telling *A* that *p*. Explicit performatives—sentences such as 'I (hereby) tell you that *p*', 'I (hereby) warn you that *p*', 'I (hereby) promise to *ψ*', 'I (hereby) request you to *ψ*', and so on—"do not 'describe' or 'report' or 'constate' anything at all, are not 'true' or 'false'."[3] (One might hold that while in uttering σ_3 *S* is not "constating" that he is telling *A* that *p*, he nevertheless means *that* he is telling *A* that *p*. Such a reply, aside from being false, would be uninteresting; for surely our inclination to say that by uttering σ_1 *S* meant that his primary intention was . . . is inextricably bound up with our inclination to say that when he uttered σ_1 *S* said *that* his primary intention was . . .) (ii) Presumably, to tell someone that *p* is (roughly) to utter *x* with the primary intention of informing someone—by means of recognition of intention—that *p*. For instance, if we know that John told Mary that Socrates was a gadfly, then we know that John uttered something intending to inform Mary—by means of recognition of intention—that Socrates was a gadfly. Evidently, then, unless 'tell' changes its meaning throughout changes of syntax, 'I hereby tell you that *p*' (σ_3) has (roughly) the same meaning as 'My primary intention in uttering this [or, 'I hereby utter this with the primary intention . . .'] is to produce in you— by means of recognition of intention—the belief (knowledge) that *p*' (σ_1). And so, presumably, what would be meant by uttering σ_1 is identical with what would be meant by uttering σ_3. And if it is true that in uttering σ_3 *S* would not mean that he was telling *A* that *p*, i.e., would not mean that he uttered σ_3 with the primary intention of informing *A* that *p* (etc.), then it would seem to follow that in uttering σ_1 *S* would not mean that his primary intention was to inform *A* (or to produce in *A* the belief) that *p* (etc.).

There are two suggestions which may be urged by way of a reply to the preceding argument. One is that in uttering an explicit performative one *does* (*pace* Austin) mean that one is performing a certain speech act, one is "constating" that one is performing a certain speech act. The other is that explicit performative verbs do in fact undergo a "change of meaning" when they occur in the first person singular present indicative active. In the next chapter I offer a detailed account of explicit performa-

3 J. L. Austin, *How to Do Things with Words*, p. 5.

tives, and these suggestions will there be discussed at some length (and dismissed). In the meantime I hope that it will be agreed that a prima facie case has been made for thinking that if *S* utters *x* with just those intentions specified in either definition, then *S* will either mean that *p* or that *A* is to *ψ*, but he will not mean anything else, no matter what he uttered.

III.3 *Alleged instances of S meaning that p and S meaning that A is to ψ where the intended response is neither the activated belief that p nor A's doing ψ*

We have now to consider certain alleged threats either to the condition that *S* meant that *p* only if *S* intended to cause in *A* the activated belief that *p* or to the condition that *S* meant that *A* was to *ψ* only if *S* intended to cause *A* to *ψ*. The allegedly problematic cases are of two types: cases in which the response *S* intends to produce in *A* is neither the activated belief that *p* nor *A*'s *ψ*-ing, and cases of utterances in the absence of an audience. The audience-less cases will be considered in section III.4.

(a) Let us begin by considering certain cases which only appear to be counter to the definitions.

(1) It has been objected that one may mean that *p* or that *A* is to *ψ* while not caring in the least whether one is believed or obeyed.

Granted that, in uttering *x*, *S* both meant that *p* and did not care whether he caused in *A* the belief that *p*. It does not follow from this that *S* did not utter *x* with the intention of causing *A* to believe that *p*.

Customer: "Where is lingerie?"
Clerk: "Lingerie is on the fifth floor."

No doubt the clerk, in saying that lingerie is on the fifth floor, intends to be complying with the cutomer's request; i.e. the clerk intends to be supplying the customer with the information requested. But it may also be that the clerk is completely indifferent to whether or not the customer accepts this information and that the clerk would not be at all disturbed were the customer to refuse to believe that lingerie is on the fifth floor.

(2) Reporter: "Tell me, Mr. President, what prompted you to lower the draft quota for November?"
Mr. President: "The election." (*Sotto voce*: "I didn't want to let that out!")

Here the speaker "blurts out" something which he intended *not* to divulge. It may seem that while the speaker succeeded in telling *A* that *p* (and, *a fortiori*, in meaning that *p*), he did not utter what he uttered intending to inform *A* that *p*.[4]

I believe that the correct and natural thing to say about this type of case is that *S* uttered *x* with the *momentary* intention of informing *A* that *p*, but that this was an intention he intended not to have. That is, *S* forgot his *standing* intention not to inform *A* that *p* and uttered *x* with the momentary intention of informing *A* that *p*. This is not an uncommon phenomenon. One who has given up smoking may, in a moment of forgetfulness, begin to smoke a cigarette. In one sense the smoker intended not to smoke the cigarette, although this was, in another sense, the intention he had in lighting the cigarette. In other words, he had an intention he intended not to have.

(3) There are cases where *S* both means that *p* (or that *A* is to *ψ*) by uttering *x* and utters *x* believing (or even knowing) that he will not thereby cause *A* to have in mind the belief that *p* (or to *ψ*), either because *S* believes that *A* already believes (and has in mind) that *p* (or has already *ψ*-ed) or because *S* believes that *A* will refuse to believe that *p* (or to *ψ*).

In general, one cannot do an act *X* with the intention of bringing about a certain result if one knows or believes that one will not thereby bring about that result. But while this is generally the case, it is not necessarily the case. A person trapped in a burning building might leap from a seventh floor window with the intention of saving his life. Somewhat analogously, it is not uncommon to try to convince someone that *p* despite its being virtually certain that one will fail.

(b) However, there are various types of cases of which one would be inclined to say that *S* meant that *p* (or that *A* was to *ψ*) even though it is quite clear that *S* had no intention to cause in *A* the activated belief that *p* (or to cause *A* to *ψ*).

(1) The Berkeley police, thinking that the campus would be the best place to contain a riot, announce to the Berkeley radicals that under no circumstances are they, the radicals, to hold their rally on the campus. It is the intention of the police that this announcement should cause the rally to be held on campus. It is clear that the police intend the radicals to *think* that they are being ordered not to meet on campus. One may also feel

---

[4] I owe this type of example to Professor P. F. Strawson.

that they *are* ordering this (and so do mean that the rally is not to be held on campus). In this case, as in all cases involving a counter-suggestible audience, S's intention in uttering x is to bring about a certain response by means of deceiving A into thinking that S uttered x intending to bring about some contrary response.

> (2) Teacher: "Tell me, if you can, when the Battle of Hastings was fought."
> Student: "1066."

Certainly it is not part of the student's intention to secure that his teacher has in mind the date of the battle. The point of both the teacher's "request" and the student's "reply" is that the student should do what he would do were he actually intending to inform (tell) the teacher of the date of the battle, thereby enabling the teacher to determine whether he does in fact know when the battle was fought. In the "counter-suggestible" example S pretended to be uttering x with certain intentions in order to deceive A into thinking that he uttered x with those intentions. In the present example S openly makes as if to be telling A that p in order to show A that he, S, is able to tell someone, and so knows, that p.

> (3) Police: "O.K., Capone, the jig's up. We know you stole the bubble-gum, so you'd better confess."
> Capone: "I confess. I stole the bubble-gum."

Here, unlike the preceding two cases, it is not entirely obvious what S's overt intention is. One may have evidence that p sufficient to warrant one's claiming to know that p, but if it is important that one be as certain that p as possible and if one's evidence is indirect, there may be a point to seeking further evidence. Since Capone is in the best possible position to know what he did, his intention in "confessing" that he stole the bubble-gum may have been to make available the best grounds for entitling the police to claim to know that he stole the bubble-gum. This is especially plausible in the present example, where Capone's utterance may be cited in court as evidence of his guilt.

But there are other "confession" cases which do not so neatly fit this explanation, e.g. George Washington's confession that he chopped down the cherry tree (when it was perfectly obvious that he did). George Washington's "confession' may have been a gesture to show that he was not dishonest, or that he was not intending to hold anything back.

> (4) Mr. Smith: "I was working in the office all evening."
> Mrs. Smith: "You're lying."

Apparently, it is not Mrs. Smith's intention to cause her husband to have in mind the fact that he is lying. More likely, her intention is to let him know that she knows that he is lying. Perhaps in such cases one gains a certain emphasis by using a sentence conventionally designed for informing someone that *p* (in this case, that one is lying).

I am inclined to think that none of these cases present a serious problem and that the sense in which it may be said of *S* in these examples that he meant that *p* or meant that *A* was to *Ψ* is an extended or attenuated sense, one derived from and dependent upon the primary sense captured in the definitions.

(1) "Counter-suggestive utterances". There are several reasons for wanting to say that it is only in an attenuated sense that the police "meant" that the rally was not to be held on campus. First, the very possibility of this type of deception is dependent upon its being *at least* generally the case that one who means that *A* is to *ψ* intends *A* to *ψ*. Unless the imperative mood were conventionally correlated with an intention to produce action, it would not be possible to pretend by uttering an imperative that one had such an intention. "Counter-suggestive" utterances, then, are directly parasitic upon primary and standard acts of meaning. Second, there is a tendency to speak of *pretended* or *as if* X-ing as X-ing, especially in those cases where what one *does* is exactly the same as what one would do were one actually X-ing (in our case, meaning such-and-such). For example, in the primary sense of the expression 'applying artificial respiration', one is applying artificial respiration to another only if one's intention in doing whatever it is that one does is to restore a person to normal breathing, but in a first-aid class the instructor might quite naturally request one student to apply artificial respiration to another student. Third, one will be willing to say that the police *meant* that the rally was not to be held on campus only in so far as one is willing to say that the police *ordered* the rally not to be held on campus. Whatever one's intuitions about

meaning, it seems more difficult to deny that in uttering *x S ordered A* to *ψ* only if *S* uttered *x* with the intention of getting *A* to *ψ*. Finally, it is worth noting that, should it be desirable, the definitions of '*S* meant that *p*' and '*S* meant that *A* was to *ψ*' may easily be altered to accommodate both the primary cases and the "counter-suggestive" cases: we simply require only that *S* utter *x* intending *A* to *think S* uttered *x* with those intentions specified in the definitions. But once such degenerate cases have been noticed and accounted for it is probably best to leave the formal definitions unaltered so that they will provide a schema more directly for the standard and primary cases.

(2) "Examination answer". Much of what was said about the preceding type of case applies to the student's "telling" his teacher that the Battle of Hastings was fought in 1066. In the primary sense of 'tell', *S told A* that *p* only if *S* uttered *x* intending to inform *A* that *p*. The student, in uttering '1066', acts *as if* he were genuinely telling the teacher when the battle was fought, and it is in virtue of this fact that we speak of the student "telling" his teacher that the Battle of Hastings was fought in 1066 and, *a fortiori*, of his meaning that the Battle of Hastings was fought in 1066. (Notice that, in appropriate circumstances, the teacher might have requested the student to "remind" (or "point out" to) him when the battle was fought.)

(3) "Confessions". Certain of these cases may be construed as meeting the conditions for *S* meaning that *p* (e.g., where *S* intends his utterance to be used by others as evidence that *p*), and others may be provided for by a slight adjustment which allows that *S* may mean that *p* when his primary intention is to strengthen an already existing belief that *p*. (There are analogous imperative cases where *S*'s primary intention is to strengthen an already existing intention; e.g., *S* orders *A* to *ψ*, which *A* was intending to do anyway, so that *A* may have additional reason to *ψ*.) More problematic are those cases of "confession" where, evidently, *S*'s intention is neither to create, activate nor strengthen a belief that *p*. My inclination is to say that here, too, our willingness to say that *S* "meant" that *p* derives from the fact that in this type of case (e.g., George Washington's "confession" that he chopped down the cherry tree) *S* utters *x* as if he were informing (telling) *A* that *p*. Communicating that *p* is a paradigm of bringing the fact that *p* "out in the open", and by acting as though he were communicating that he did such-and-such the confessor

purports to show that he is willing to have it out in the open that he did such-and-such.

(4) "Accusations". While it is true that Mrs. Smith meant that she knew (or believed) that her husband was lying, it is, strictly speaking, false that she meant that he was lying. Such cases are not unlike the "examination answer" cases: *S* shows that he knows that *p* by uttering a sentence which he would utter were he to inform someone that *p*.

III.4 *Instances of S-meaning in the absence of an audience*

These cases divide into two types: (a) those in which *S* utters *x* because of the possibility of producing a certain response in some person or type of person, and (b) those cases in which *S* utters *x* without having (or without seeming to have) any audience-directed intention at all.

(a) Examples of the first type are:

(i) *S*, on the off-chance that his mother-in-law will stop by, leaves a note on the door telling her that he will be away for the evening.

(ii) *S* records in his private diary that his mother-in-law stopped by for the tenth consecutive evening. (Presumably, *S* feels that his future self may be sufficiently interested in being reminded or told of what transpired in his younger days.)

(iii) Fearing that hippies may discover his land and take to camping on it, *S* posts a sign saying, "Private property. Keep out".[5]

This range of examples poses three minor problems for the definitions of '*S* meant that *p*' and '*S* meant that *A* was to *ψ*'.

(1) The first difficulty arises over the description of *S*'s primary intention. In example (i), for instance, should we say that *S*'s primary intention is to inform his mother-in-law that he is away for the evening, or should we only say that his primary intention is to inform his mother-in-law that he is away *if* she happens by (or, that he left the note intending that, should she happen by, she will be informed that he is away)?

If *S* utters *x* with the intention of thereby informing *A* that *p*, there are several ways in which he might fail to achieve this end: *A* might already know that *p*; *A* might refuse to believe that *p*; or *A* might not encounter *S*'s utterance *x*. Generally, if *S* utters

---

5 This example was suggested by an example of Grice's in "Utterer's Meaning and Intentions", p. 172.

x with the intention of informing *A* that *p*, *S* will expect to inform *A* that *p*; but we have already noticed that *S* may be said to intend to inform *A* that *p* even though he may think that *A* already knows that *p* and even though he may think that *A* will probably refuse to believe that *p*. The case where *S* utters *x* thinking that *A* will probably not encounter *x* does not seem relevantly different, and so, by parity of reason, the fact that there is a good chance that *S*'s utterance will go unnoticed does not seem to be sufficient to defeat the claim that he uttered *x* intending to inform *A* that *p*. I think this position is supported by our normal way of describing such cases. For example, we may say that a person's intention in putting a fence around a pit was to prevent someone's falling in, despite the fact that it was known to be highly unlikely that anyone would go near the pit.

The next two difficulties have to do with the mutual knowledge* conditions, and they will require slight revision.

(2) Consider again example (i). Since *S* will not know if his mother-in-law sees the note, he cannot have intended by putting up the note to realize a state of affairs *E* which is such that if *E* obtains, then he and his mother-in-law will mutually know* that it obtains.

But suppose that *S*'s mother-in-law does encounter the note. She will then know that he knows that the note is on the door; she will then know that he knows that if she knows that the note is on the door, then she will know that he knows that the note is on the door; she will then know that he knows that if she knows that the note is on the door, then she will know that he knows that if she knows that the note is on the door, then she will know that he knows that the note is on the door; and so on, *ad infinitum.*

For this type of case, then, we may say that

S uttered *x* intending thereby to realize a certain state of affairs *E* which is (intended by *S* to be) such that if *E* obtains, then

(1a) if *A* knows that *E* obtains, then *A* will know that *S* knows that *E* obtains;

(1b) if *A* knows that *E* obtains, then *A* will know that *S* knows that (1a);

(1c) if *A* knows that *E* obtains, then *A* will know that *S* knows that (1b); and so on.

(That is,

$$K_A E \rightarrow K_A K_S E \ \&$$
$$K_A K_S (K_A E \rightarrow K_A K_S E) \ \&$$
$$K_A K_S (K_A E \rightarrow K_A K_S (K_A E \rightarrow K_A K_S E)) \ \&$$

.

.

.)

(3) In example (iii) S's intention is not to produce a response in a particular person A, but only to produce a certain response in *any person* of a certain type. Consider another example with this feature. S places a "car for sale" notice in a newspaper intending to inform anyone reading the paper of this fact. Obviously, it would be false to say that Smith, who placed the advertisement, and Angleworm, who read it, mutually know* about the advertisement; for it may well be that Smith is completely ignorant of Angleworm's existence. In this case, there is a certain property F such that Smith places the advertisement intending to realize a certain state of affairs E which is such that if E obtains, then

(1a) if anyone who is F [e.g., anyone who reads the advertisement] knows that E obtains, then that person will know that S knows that E obtains;

(1b) if anyone who is F knows that E obtains, then that person will know that S knows that (1a); and so on.

A moment's reflection shows that in all instances of S-meaning (so far considered, at least) S's intention may be so described. For example, S may intend to produce a certain response in anyone who is identical with Angleworm, or anyone who is the one and only man standing immediately before him, etc.

We arrive, then, at the following (quite informal) redefinitions which should accommodate all of the cases considered so far.

S meant that p by uttering x iff S uttered x intending thereby to realize a certain state of affairs E which is (intended by S to be) such that the obtainment of E is sufficient to secure that

(1a) if anyone who has a certain property F knows that E obtains, then that person will know that S knows that E obtains;

(1b) if anyone who is F knows that E obtains, then that person will know that S knows that (1a); and so on;

(2a) if anyone who is F knows that E obtains, then that person will know (or believe)—and know that S knows (or believes)—that E is conclusive (very good or good) evidence that S uttered x with the primary intention

(1′) that there be some ρ such that S's utterance of x causes in anyone who is F the activated belief that $p/\rho(t)$;

and intending

(2′) satisfaction of (1′) to be achieved, at least in part, by virtue of that person's [i.e., the person(s) satisfying (1′)] belief that x is related in a certain way R to the belief that p;

(3′) to realize E;

(2b) if anyone who is F knows that E obtains, then that person will know that S knows that (2a); and so on.

Likewise for the analysans for the account of what it is for S to mean that A [or anyone who is F] is to ψ.

The definitions on page 63 are seen to be a consequence of the above redefinitions once it is specified that S uttered x in the presence of the intended audience, and for all practical purposes the definitions on page 63 will continue to serve as models for the standard and primary case.

(b) We turn now to the alleged cases of S meaning that p or S meaning that A is to ψ where there is no audience-directed intention at all.

To begin with it is relevant to recall the distinction made in section I.1 between the two senses in which a person may be said to have meant something. For many of the cases cited as presenting a difficulty for the condition in question are cases where it is true to say that, for example, by 'The cat is on the mat' S meant "The cat is on the mat", but not true to say that in uttering 'The cat is on the mat' S meant *that* the cat was on the mat. One might, for some reason or other, while alone and in the privacy of one's study, write out the entire text of *Mr. Apollinax*. No doubt one will have meant something by the words 'He laughed like an irresponsible foetus', but it is unlikely that in writing this one will have meant 1*that* . . . What we want to find are examples of S

meaning that *p* or examples of *S* meaning that *A* is to ψ where *S* has no intention to produce a response in some actual or possible audience (including himself on some later occasion).

Such examples are not, I think, easy to come by. I have neither heard nor (with one possible exception to be mentioned later) been able myself to think of any examples of this type of which it may plausibly be said that in uttering *x S* meant that so-and-so was to ψ. It is not quite as difficult to find candidate examples for the case of *S* meaning that *p*.

(i) A philosopher, alone and in the privacy of his study, is determined to get somewhere on a certain philosophical problem, for example about the relation between meaning and intention. Toward this end he writes down various arguments, suggestions, objections, replies, etc. For example, at one point he writes, "If we should learn that the members of a certain tribe utter the sound 'gavagai' *whenever* a rabbit is present, then the last thing we should say is that in uttering 'gavagai' they mean that a rabbit is present."

Let us suppose that the philosopher has no intention of showing his notes to anyone or of consulting them himself on some later occasion. His intention is to discover the truth.

(ii) A man, during his deliberations about whether to marry Rose, makes a list of her pros and cons. We might suppose that in writing 'She has halitosis' he meant that she had halitosis.

What should we say about these examples?

(1) We might simply deny that we have here instances of *S* meaning that *p* by uttering *x*. Is it really clear that in (or by) writing 'She has halitosis' *S* meant *that* she had halitosis? Suppose that instead of writing anything down *S* only put together these thoughts in his head. Here it seems to me even less plausible to say that *S* meant that Rose had halitosis when he, as it were, ran the sentence 'She has halitosis' through his mind. But then why should the fact that he did not actually write or utter aloud the sentence constitute a relevant difference?

However, I fear that taking this way out would not win many converts, and for at least this reason I shall henceforth assume that we do want to say of these cases that in uttering *x S* meant that *p*. Another reason for dismissing this hard line is that there is *some* inclination to say that *S* meant that *p*, and this is worth accounting for.

(2) One possible way of accounting for these cases is suggested and illuminated by an analogy with, of all things, jokes. It would appear to be eminently reasonable to think that an utterance-token x is a *joke*—in the primary and important sense of that word—only if someone uttered x intending thereby to amuse someone. But we can easily imagine a dour man, alone in his study, writing 'My wife is so skinny she has to walk around in the shower to get wet' with the intention of writing down a joke, and this despite the fact that he has no intention of amusing himself—at that or some later time—or anyone else. Here we are willing to say that S's utterance x is a "joke" in virtue of his uttering x with the intention of uttering something which *would* amuse a certain type of audience (if uttered in certain (types of) circumstances).

Similarly, it may be that we are inclined to say of S in examples (i) and (ii) that he meant that p by uttering x in virtue of his uttering x with the intention of uttering something which *would* produce the belief (or activated belief) that p (in the appropriate way, etc.) in a certain type of audience if uttered in circumstances of a certain type. Thus, while in example (i) S does not actually intend to *convince* anyone that p, he may nevertheless criticize the arguments he produces for not being *convincing*.

While an explanation of this sort may account for part of what we have in mind when, of such cases, we say that S meant that p, it cannot be a complete explanation; for there are cases where S utters x intending that his utterance x be such that it would produce the relevant sort of response (in the relevant way) in a certain type of audience, but where it is false that S meant something by uttering x. I do not, for example, think that S meant that p or that S meant that A was to ψ in either of the following two examples.

(iii) A sadistic lieutenant, realizing that he has in his command a naïve and overzealous private, takes delight, while alone, in saying aloud, "Private Goodfellow, run your bayonet through your abdomen, and look sharp about it!", knowing that were he to utter this in Goodfellow's presence, Goodfellow would do just that. But it would be a perversion of our intuitions about meaning to say that the lieutenant meant by his utterance that Goodfellow was to run the bayonet through his abdomen.

(iv) A purist, determined never to produce a false sentence, practises on his typewriter by typing the sentence 'Snow is white'.

Since his intention is to produce a true sentence, his intention, presumably, is to produce something which could be used to tell someone that snow is white. Notwithstanding this, it is false that in typing 'Snow is white' he meant that snow was white.

(3) What is the relevant difference between, on the one hand, examples (i) and (ii), where we are inclined to say that *S* meant that *p* and, on the other hand, examples (iii) and (iv), where we are not so inclined? I should like to suggest that audience-less examples of types (i) and (ii) are not so very different after all from those cases where there clearly is an intention to produce a response in some audience.

Recall the reasons for thinking that in examples (i) and (ii) *S* does not intend to produce in anyone the activated belief that *p*: it is clear that since *S* already has in mind the belief that *p* when he utters *x*, he cannot, in uttering *x*, intend to produce in himself that response, and since we may suppose that *S* destroyed what he wrote immediately after his writing session, he cannot have intended the sentence-tokens he produced to cause a response in himself or another on some future occasion.

But consider example (i). *S* writes down various things intending to arrive at an argument to establish that *p*. It is not incompatible with the description of this example that *S*'s primary intention was to arrive at an argument which could be *reproduced* to convince a certain type of audience that *p*. Indeed, the academic life being what it is, this may be the most plausible description of *S*'s intention. But it would be unduly philistine to think that this is always one's intention in such cases. One might want to do philosophy even though locked in solitary confinement for life.

But it does seem essential to the "philosophy" example that *S*'s intention is to *provide himself* with various arguments, explanations, etc. In this type of case *S* does not have various arguments, etc., all worked out which he then simply puts on paper (that would be like the "typing" example); rather, he puts various things on paper as part of a process toward arriving at a certain body of *knowledge*. In the audience-present cases of this type *S*'s intention is to provide another with certain arguments, explanations, etc.; in the audience-less cases of this type *S*'s intention is to provide himself with certain arguments, explanations, etc.

Example (ii) is the audience-less analogue of the "fact review" example described in section II.3. There *S* uttered 'Rose earns 30 pounds a week . . .' with the intention of securing that *A* has all of the relevant facts about Rose in mind while reaching a decision as to whether he should marry her. In example (ii) *S* is doing this job for himself.

I submit, then, that in each case where it is both the case that we are inclined to say that *S* meant that *p* by uttering *x* and that *S* apparently had no audience-directed intention, *S*'s utterance *x* will be part of some activity directed towards securing some cognitive response in himself, and that it is in virtue of this significant resemblance to the standard case that we class these cases as instances of *S*-meaning.

I mentioned above that it is extremely difficult to find examples of the relevant sort where we would be inclined to say that *S* meant that so-and-so was to *ψ*. The following example may be an exception. Suppose I am planning a bank robbery. I want to secure that I have a complete plan in mind when I undertake this endeavour, and towards this end I write down, 'First, knock out alarm system; second, shoot guard . . .'. Here it does not seem too unnatural to say that I meant that I was first to knock out the alarm system, etc., and this is so because my intention in writing what I wrote was to secure that I would have in mind a network of intentions.

The proffered explanation of audience-less cases also accounts for why it is difficult to find examples where we would be willing to say that *S* meant that *A* was to *ψ* and why we are not inclined to say that *S* meant something by uttering *x* in examples (iii) and (iv).

III.5 *S meant something by uttering x*

Finally, there remains to be defined '*S* meant something by (or in) uttering *x*'. Two complementary arguments will be given to show that *S* meant something by uttering *x* if and only if, for some *p*, *A* [or *F*], and *ψ*, by uttering *x* *S* meant that *p* or *S* meant that *A* [or anyone who was *F*] was to *ψ*. (The qualification in brackets should be understood throughout.)

The first argument is designed to show that if *S* utters *x* with the intention of thereby producing a certain response *r* in an audience *A*, then *S* will mean something by uttering *x* *only if*, for some *p* and some *ψ*, the response *r* is *A*'s (actively) thinking that p or is A's doing ψ; i.e., if S utters x with the primary intention of producing in A a certain response r and if the value of 'r' is anything other than a belief or action, then S will not have meant anything by uttering x (unless, of course, S also uttered x with a primary intention to produce in A the activated belief that p or a primary intention to get A to ψ). If this can be shown, then, given that to mean something S must intend to produce some response in an audience and given the correctness of the definitions of 'S meant that p' and 'S meant that A was to ψ', it will follow that S meant something by uttering x if and only if, for some p, A, and ψ, by uttering x S meant that p or S meant that A was to ψ.

The second argument proceeds primarily by way of showing that if S utters a well-formed sentence of English with that sentence's full conventional force, then, for some p, A, and ψ, S will mean thereby either that p or that A is to ψ.

First argument

Consider the following cases.

(i) S snubs A in the street, intending thereby to cause A to be distressed. (This example is the only explicit reason given by Grice for allowing affective attitudes into his account of S-meaning: "if I cut someone in the street I do feel inclined to assimilate this to cases of meaning$_{nn}$, and this inclination seems to me dependent on the fact that I could not reasonably expect him to be distressed (indignant, humiliated) unless he recognized my intention to affect him in this way."[6])

(ii) S does the washing-up to please his wife. Since his doing the washing-up will please her only if it is done to please her, he intends her to recognize his intention to please her.

(iii) S utters x with the intention of causing—by means of recognition of intention—A to be afraid of a certain dog, Fido.[7] More specifically, S intends A to recognize S's intention to get A to fear Fido and to have this as his reason for being afraid of Fido.

If feeling distressed, pleased, or afraid were relevant responses for an account of S-meaning, then it would be the case both that (1) S meant something in one or more of the examples (i)–(iii) and (2) *what S meant* [for convenience, Φ] is such that S's intention to cause A distress (pleasure, or fear)—in a certain way,

---

[6] "Meaning", p. 384.

[7] By using 'x' rather than some sentence I am being charitable.

etc.—is either a sufficient condition for S meaning Φ or a necessary condition for S meaning Φ (or a necessary part of a sufficient but not necessary condition for S meaning Φ, etc., although this much caution will not be necessary). (Clearly, it is not enough that S meant something in each (or any) of the above examples. First, if S meant something, then there is (as it were) something that S meant. Second, it may be that while S meant something by uttering x he meant something as a result, say, of his intention to produce in A the belief that p and not in virtue of his intention to cause A to be afraid. For example, a second might shout "Get angry!" to his lugubrious prize-fighter, and here the second would have meant that the prize-fighter was to make himself angry; but he would have meant this in virtue of his intention to cause A to *make himself* angry and not in virtue of his intention to produce the response of anger.)

What, if anything, does S mean in example (i)? A plausible answer is that S meant that he was through with A (this is in fact the answer given to me by Grice when I asked him this question). But if the definition of 'S meant that p' is correct, then the only response relevant for S meaning that he is through with A is A thinking that S is through with him. Example (i) gives us no reason to doubt this result, for S could not have intended to cause A distress unless he intended to cause A to think that S was through with him. (It may be that A would not think that S intended to produce in A the belief that he, S, was through with A unless A thought that S intended to cause A distress, but that is irrelevant.)

Similar conclusions are reached with regard to examples (ii) and (iii). If S meant anything by washing-up it was that he wanted to please his wife, or that he was doing the washing-up in order to please her. Likewise, in example (iii) S either meant that Fido was dangerous or that there was reason to fear Fido or that A should be on guard against Fido or, conceivably, that A was to make himself afraid of Fido. But no matter which of these things S meant, it is both necessary and sufficient (given, of course, satisfaction of all relevant conditions) for S meaning what he meant that the intended response be A's (actively) thinking that p or else A's doing ψ.

Should the preceding be correct, we may conclude that neither distress nor pleasure nor fear is a relevant response; and there is reason to think that this conclusion may be extended to encompasss all affective attitudes and emotions. First, I submit that if the reader considers any example in which S utters x intending to produce an affective response in A, then, should S mean anything by uttering x, the reader will find either that, for some p, S means that p or that, for some ψ, S means that A is to ψ (at least this has been my experience). Secondly, it seems implausible that what should apply to distress, pleasure, and fear with regard to meaning should not apply as well to any other affective attitude or emotion. And since other types of propositional attitudes—e.g., doubting, suspecting—are definable in terms of belief or intention, we seem, as intended, to be left with only belief and action (intention) as the only relevant types of response.

If it is true that one can mean something only in virtue of an intention to produce (activated) belief or an intention to produce action, then there should be some important difference between believing and intending and all other types of responses for which one may have reasons (viz., affective attitudes and some emotions). I believe that the relevant difference is one noticed by Grice in "Meaning". Grice pointed out that "to have a reason for believing so-and-so . . . is . . . like 'having a motive for' accepting so-and-so", and that decisions "that" seem to involve decisions "to", but that "one cannot in any straightforward sense 'decide' to be offended" (p. 386). Thus the relevant difference between beliefs and actions, on the one hand, and affective attitudes on the other may be that the elements of deliberation and decision are absent in the case of affective attitudes. When all the facts are known, one may deliberate about whether or not one should believe that p or about whether or not one should ψ. But when all of the relevant facts are known one either hates Angleworm or one does not. It would be most odd for one to ponder, "Well, Angleworm slandered my wife, is generally odious and malicious. Should I hate him?" (There is a sense in which one might ask "Should I be angry with him?" But such a question most naturally arises, e.g., when one isn't sure how one is to take what someone said or did, and this is a case where all of the relevant facts are not known.)

Second argument

Let 'σ' stand for any well-formed English sentence. I want to say that if S utters σ with its full conventional force, then, for some p, A, and ψ, what S will mean by (or in) uttering σ is either that p or else that A is to ψ. Before arguing for this a few preliminary comments will be useful.

(1) I shall use the word 'sentence' in such a way that 'The cat is on the mat.' is a sentence, but 'the cat is on the mat' is not a sentence. (In speech this distinction is marked by pauses, intonation, linguistic context, etc.)

(2) "Full conventional force." For example, S utters 'The cat is on the mat.' with its "full conventional force" (roughly) if and only if S utters 'The cat is on the mat.' and means thereby that the cat is on the mat. If, say, S utters 'The cat is on the mat.' and means "The cat is on the mat" by 'The cat is on the mat.' (as has been true of me in using this sentence as an example) but does not mean by uttering 'The cat is on the mat.' that the cat is on the mat, then S has not uttered 'The cat is on the mat.' with its full conventional force. Loosely speaking, to utter σ with its full conventional force is to utter σ and to mean thereby what one says. So, again loosely speaking, I want to say that if S utters a well-formed English sentence and means what he says, then, for some p and some ψ, he will either mean that p or else he will mean that so-and-so is to ψ. (For convenience, I ignore problems of ambiguity.)

(3) I do not maintain that if asked what S meant by uttering σ one must reply by *saying* that he meant that p (or that A was to ψ). One might reply in all sorts of ways: "He said that p"; "He asked whether p"; "He meant the cat was on the mat"; etc. However, I do want to say that in so far as these replies are genuine replies, then they will entail that S meant that p (or that S meant that A was to ψ).

The argument is quite simple.

(i) If σ is a well-formed English sentence, then (roughly but not too roughly speaking) σ will be in the indicative, subjunctive, optative, imperative, or interrogative mood. (This is a more generous use of 'mood' than most grammarians would allow, but that is irrelevant.)

(ii) If σ is in the indicative mood and if S utters σ with its full conventional force, then, for some p, S will mean that p by (or in) uttering σ (and, in the absence of further intentions, S will not mean anything else by uttering σ; this rider should be understood throughout). For example, if S utters 'It is raining.' with its full conventional force, then S will mean that it is raining. On the whole this is obvious enough, but there may seem to be a difficulty with explicit performatives. However, in Chapter IV I shall argue that if, say, *S* were, *per impossibile*, to utter 'I request you to pass the salt.' with its full conventional force, then he would mean thereby that he is requesting *A* to pass the salt. (As suggested in section III.2, meaning being what it is, *S cannot* mean that he is requesting *A* to pass the salt.)

(iii) If σ is in the subjunctive mood and if *S* utters σ with its full conventional force, then, for some *p*, *S* will mean that *p* by (or in) uttering σ. For example, if *S* utters 'If the cat had been on the mat, then hairs would not be on the floor.' and means what he says, then *S* will mean that if the cat had been on the mat, then hairs would not be on the floor.

(iv) If σ is in the optative mood and if *S* utters σ with its full conventional force, then, for some *p*, *S* will mean that *p* by (or in) uttering σ. Thus, if *S* utters 'Would that my own true love were in my arms!' and means what he says, then he means that he wishes that his own true love were in his arms. (Such a sentence, if uttered at all, would perhaps be uttered as a "pure expression of feeling"; but in this case σ would not have been uttered with its full conventional force and *S* would not have meant anything by uttering σ.)

(v) If σ is in the imperative mood and if *S* utters σ with its full conventional force, then, for some *A* and some ψ, by (or in) uttering σ *S* will mean that *A* is to ψ. For example, in uttering 'Shut the door!' *S* meant that John was to shut the door.

(vi) If σ is in the interrogative mood and if *S* utters σ with its full conventional force, then, for some *A* and some ψ, by (or in) uttering σ *S* will mean that *A* is to ψ. Questions, I want to say, are requests for information. So if I ask you what time it is I am requesting you to tell me the time. If I ask you whether or not snow is white, then I am requesting you to inform me of whether or not snow is white. If we were to analyse questions in terms of force or mood indicating device plus propositional content or sentence radical, then we would (essentially) represent 'What time is it?' as

! [your informing me of the time];

and we would (essentially) represent so-called "yes-no" questions, such as 'Is it raining'?, as

! [your informing me of whether or not it is raining].

I believe that apart from any particular theory of *S*-meaning this account of interrogatives is plausible; but—taking into account the principle that if the only difference between two utterances is that in one case *S* utters *x* and in the other *y*, then what *S* meant by uttering *x* was identical with what *S* meant by uttering *y*—we have a special reason: if I utter 'What time is it?' with its full conventional force, then I will utter it with (roughly) the intention of thereby getting *A*—by means of recognition of intention—to inform me of the time, and if I utter 'Inform me of the time, please.' with its full conventional force, then I will utter it with (roughly) the intention of getting *A*—by means of recognition of intention—to inform me of the time; and since the only difference between the "question" and the "request" is in the type of sentence uttered (the means used to make known my intentions), there will be no difference in what I meant.

So we have the conclusion that if *S* utters σ and means what he says, then, for some p, *A*, and ψ, by (or in) uttering σ *S* will either mean that p or else he will mean that *A* is to ψ. This is not yet enough to give us the conclusion that *S* meant something by (or in) uttering *x* if and only if, for some p, *A*, and ψ, by (or in) uttering *x* *S* meant that p or *S* meant that *A* was to ψ. We will get that desired result with the addition of the following premiss, which, strictly, is more than is needed.

Let 'Φ' be a "dummy" for any expression which can complete the sentence form '*S* meant that . . . by (or in) uttering *x*'. If by uttering *x* *S* meant that Φ, then there is some (English) sentence σ such that if *S* utters σ with its full conventional force, then *S* will mean that Φ by uttering σ. (This premiss expresses the belief that whatever can be meant can be said. I do not know how to prove this assumption, but given the general thesis about meaning and language being proffered, it is not difficult to think of reasons why this premiss should be true.) This, together with the premiss that if *S* utters σ with its full conventional force, then, for some p, *A*, and ψ, by uttering σ *S* will mean that p or else *S* will mean that *A* is to ψ, yields the conclusion that *S* meant something by uttering *x* if and only if, for some p, *A*, and ψ, by uttering *x* *S* meant that p or *S* meant that *A* was to ψ.

There is one consequence of this definition of '*S* meant something by uttering *x*' worth mentioning. It is an essential part of the Austin–Wittgenstein legacy that the class of utterances does not neatly and simply divide into two jointly exhaustive and mutually exclusive subclasses: "statements" and "imperatives". If what I have said in this section is correct, there is very good reason to think that this legacy is false. More will be said about this in the next chapter.

IV

S-MEANING AND SPEECH ACTS

IV.1 *Austin's theory of locutionary, illocutionary and perlocutionary acts*

I F one takes seriously the idea that knowing a language is knowing how to do things with words, then a natural question to ask is: What things? What kinds of acts are essential to, or constitutive of, language use? As money is used to buy things with, so words are used to . . .? To answer this question it is necessary to study the total speech act in the total speech situation, and this is what Austin is concerned to do in *How to Do Things with Words*. The answer was meant to be provided by way of Austin's thesis that there are three types of acts standardly performed when one uses language: locutionary, illocutionary, and perlocutionary acts. These three types of acts are characterized by Austin in the following way.

(a) A *locutionary act* is an act *of* saying something, and to perform an act of saying something—in the full normal sense of 'saying something'—involves uttering noises (the "phonetic" act) of certain types belonging to and as belonging to a certain vocabulary, conforming to and as conforming to a certain grammar (the "phatic" act), and with a certain sense and reference, which together are equivalent to meaning (the "rhetic" act) (Austin, op. cit., pp. 92–8, 108). Austin also seems to suggest that what locutionary act a person performed when he uttered a certain sentence is determined by what he meant by that sentence (ibid., pp. 98, 100). Presumably, then, to know what *S* meant by a sentence σ is to know what he said in uttering σ. But Austin's concern with both the locutionary and perlocutionary act is principally to distinguish them from the illocutionary act, with which he is primarily concerned, and he remarks that further refinements would be necessary were he to discuss the locutionary act for its own sake (ibid., pp. 94–5, 103). I will have something more to say about locutionary acts in section IV.4.

(b) Generally, to perform a locutionary act is also and *eo ipso* to perform an *illocutionary act* (ibid., p. 98). Austin does not explicitly define 'illocutionary act'; indeed, he suggests that the class of kinds of illocutionary acts is not one that can be clearly defined (ibid., p. 99). But we can gather from what he says certain criteria which provide, separately, either a necessary or a sufficient condition for at least the identification of a kind of act as a kind of illocutionary act.

(1) An illocutionary act is an act one performs *in* saying something, as opposed to an act *of* saying something (e.g., "in saying . . . he was warning you that . . .") (ibid.). There are certain illocutionary acts which can be performed by non-verbal means (e.g., warning and protesting), but even here the illocutionary act is an act one performs *in* doing something (e.g., in waving a stick or in throwing a tomato) (ibid., p. 118). However, not every act one may perform in saying something is an illocutionary act. For example, joking, showing off, and insinuating may be done in saying something, but they are not illocutionary acts (ibid., pp. 104–5, 121).

(2) To know what illocutionary act was performed in saying such-and-such, it may not be enough, and usually is not enough, to know what was meant by the sentence uttered: one must also know what it was meant *as* (e.g., whether 'It's going to charge' was meant as a prediction or warning); one must know how the locution *ought to be taken* (e.g., whether it ought to be taken as a prediction or guess) (ibid., pp. 98–100). But this does not provide a sufficient condition either, for one can say that a certain locution was meant as, or ought to have been taken as, a joke.

(3) A necessary condition for the happy and successful performance of an illocutionary act is that "uptake" be secured; i.e., an illocutionary act will not be successfully brought off unless the speaker brings about in his audience the understanding of the meaning and of the force of the locution (ibid., pp. 115–16). (Strawson suggests that the relation between the illocutionary force of an utterance and the illocutionary act performed in issuing the utterance may be expressed "by saying that to know the force of an utterance is the same thing as to know what illocutionary act, *if any*, was actually performed in issuing it".[1] I would also agree with Strawson's objection that the achievement of uptake is not a necessary condition for the performance of an illocutionary act (ibid., p. 448); thus, for example, it may be that *S* raised an objection to *A*'s statement, even though *A*

---

[1] "Intention and Convention in Speech Acts", p. 440.

failed to hear or understand what *S* said. In some cases, however, such as warning someone, the claim that achievement of uptake is not a necessary condition for the performance of speech acts of that kind may involve a slight element of legislation.)

(4) A sufficient but perhaps not a necessary condition for a kind of act being a kind of illocutionary act is that the verb which names that kind of act can function as an explicit performative verb (Austin, op. cit., pp. 131, 149). Thus, promising, warning, and ordering are kinds of illocutionary acts, for 'I (hereby) promise to . . .', 'I (hereby) warn you that . . .', and 'I (hereby) order you to . . .' are explicit performatives: in uttering these expressions one would be promising, warning, and ordering respectively.

(5) The illocutionary act "is a conventional act: an act done as conforming to a convention" (ibid., p. 105). Any given utterance has the force it has by virtue of "the conventions of illocutionary force as bearing on the special circumstances of the occasion of the issuing of the utterance" (ibid., p. 114). The illocutionary act is "constituted not by intention or by fact essentially, but by *convention* (which is, of course, a fact)" (ibid., p. 127). Even when an illocutionary act is performed non-verbally it is a conventional act and the means used for performing the act must be conventional (ibid., pp. 118, 120-1). Now this necessary condition—roughly, that a kind of act is a kind of illocutionary act only if acts of that kind are essentially conventional acts—has a special status *vis-à-vis* conditions (1)-(4): conditions (1)-(4) enable one to *identify* a kind of act as a kind of illocutionary act, but they do not, except superficially, provide one with an analysis of the concept of an illocutionary act. Condition (5), on the other hand, is the type of condition which might appear in an analytical account of illocutionary acts. More will be said about this shortly.

(c) Generally, when one performs an illocutionary act in saying such-and-such, one also performs a *perlocutionary act* by saying such-and-such. One performs a perlocutionary act by uttering *x* if and only if by uttering *x*, one produces, intentionally or unintentionally, certain "consequential effects upon the feelings, thoughts, or actions of the audience, or of the speaker, or of other persons . . ." (ibid., p. 101). Thus, convincing, persuading, frightening, annoying, and amusing are perlocutionary acts. Perlocutionary acts are *not* conventional acts, although one may perform a perlocutionary act by a conventional means; that is, "conventional acts may be made use of in order to bring off the perlocutionary act" (ibid., p. 120). I shall have nothing more to say about perlocutionary acts.

The key notion in Austin's theory of speech acts is, of course, his concept of the illocutionary act; but Austin did not provide us with an analysis of this concept. My primary purpose in this chapter is to offer such an analysis; so it will be well to begin with a brief discussion of Austin's claim that illocutionary acts are conventional acts.

I think that we are to understand Austin's claim that illocutionary acts are conventional acts as at least committing him to this: a kind of act X is a kind of illocutionary act *only if* there exist certain conventions such that (primarily) by virtue of these conventions the performance of certain sorts of non-conventional acts (e.g., uttering sounds of a certain type) by certain sorts of persons in certain sorts of circumstances is constituted an instance of X-ing. This, together with Austin's apparent suggestion that illocutionary acts are conventional acts in the same way that kicking a goal is a conventional act (ibid., p. 106), suggests that Austin thought illocutionary acts are made possible by conventions or rules of the type which Rawls and Searle have called "constitutive rules".[2]

I believe that it is false that illocutionary acts are conventional acts in the sense intended by Austin. Perhaps there are some speech acts—e.g., an umpire putting a runner out by uttering 'Out!'—which are conventional acts in the sense intended by Austin, but these are very special cases and of peripheral interest only; and I would agree with Strawson that in the majority of cases "it is not as conforming to an accepted *convention* of any kind (other than those linguistic conventions which help to fix the meaning of the utterance) that an illocutionary act is performed."[3] For example, in uttering the sentence 'Jones has only one leg', S may be objecting to A's statement that Jones is a nimble dancer, but that this is so would seem to be a result of the intentions with which the sentence was uttered and not a result of any conventions of illocutionary force "bearing on the special circumstances of the occasion of the issuing of the utterance".

[2] John Rawls, "Two Concepts of Rules"; John R. Searle, *Speech Acts*.
[3] "Intention and Convention in Speech Acts", p. 443.

In the second place, it should be clear that on the view of S-meaning that I have presented, acts of S-meaning are not conventional acts, although the performance of such acts is usually accomplished by the utilization of some conventional linguistic means. Acts of S-meaning, I am committed to saying, are non-conventional acts usually performed by the use of a conventional means.[4] And if the preceding two points are true, it follows, I think, that illocutionary acts are not conventional acts in the sense intended by Austin. But I shall put off further discussion of the relation between illocutionary force and convention until the next chapter.

IV.2. S-meaning and illocutionary acts

We want, then, an account of illocutionary acts that does not require that they be conventional acts. Such an account was offered by Strawson in "Intention and Convention in Speech Acts". Since Strawson's account is in terms of Grice's account of S-meaning, it will be helpful to take Strawson's account as our springboard.

Strawson first offers an account of what it is for an audience A to understand something by an utterance x complementary to Grice's account (as modified by Strawson: see section II.1) of what it is for someone S to mean something by uttering x. A tentative identification is then made of Austin's notion of uptake with this account of understanding. This identification entails a similar identification of Austin's notions of illocutionary force and illocutionary act—given the proviso that the achievement of uptake is not a necessary condition for the performance of an illocutionary act—with Grice's account of what it is for S to mean something by uttering x. Thus, according to Strawson's tentative account of illocutionary force, we get:

(a) S performed some illocutionary act in uttering x iff S uttered x intending

(1) to produce thereby a certain response r in a certain audience A;

(2) A to recognize S's intention (1);

(3) A's recognition of S's intention (1) to function as at least part of A's reason for A's response r;

(4) A to recognize S's intention (2).

---

[4] Cf. Strawson, "Intention and Convention in Speech Acts", pp. 456–7.

On Grice's account of S-meaning one knows what S meant by uttering x just in case one knows what response S intended to produce in A by means of recognition of intention. On Strawson's tentative extension of Grice's account to illocutionary force, one knows the particular illocutionary force of an utterance just in case one knows the particular response(s) S intended to produce in A by means of recognition of intention. For example, if in uttering x S intends to secure—by means of recognition of intention—that A is on guard against p-perils, then in uttering x S was warning A that p. So in addition to (a) we get:

(b) What illocutionary act(s) S performed in uttering x is determined by and only by the value(s) of 'r'.

But this tentative account is found by Strawson to be inadequate for two reasons. (1) Part (b) fails to provide a sufficient condition for the determination of the illocutionary force of an utterance. For example, S's utterance of 'Don't go away!' may have the force either of a request, of an entreaty, or of an order, although in either of these cases the primary response aimed at is that of getting A to stay where he is.[5] Strawson suggests that this variation in illocutionary force may be accommodated in his scheme by making room for a fuller specification of the reasons, in addition to recognition of intention, intended by S to be operative in securing the primary response aimed at. (2) The analysis is inapplicable in the case of illocutionary acts (if they are "illocutionary acts", see below, p. 104) which are essentially conventional; such cases, that is, as "an umpire giving a batsman out, a jury bringing in a verdict of guilty, a judge pronouncing sentence, a player redoubling at bridge, a priest or a civil officer pronouncing a couple man and wife". In such cases, Strawson suggests, condition (1) of part (a), the intention to secure a certain response (over and above the securing of uptake) in a certain audience must be dropped. "It is not even possible, in other than a formal sense, to isolate, among all the participants in the procedure (trial, marriage, game) to which the utterance belongs, a particular audience to whom the utterance can be said to be addressed."[6]

But such speech acts as belong to highly conventionalized institutions are, from the point of view of the theory of language and communication, of marginal interest only. The primary and

⁵ Ibid., pp. 454–5.   ⁶ Ibid., p. 456.

important case is that of the kind of illocutionary act which is not essentially conventional, and it follows from Strawson's argument that part (a) of his analysis may be thought of as providing necessary and perhaps sufficient conditions for performing a standard non-conventional illocutionary act.[7] Part (b), of course, must be revised to accommodate the first objection to Strawson's tentative account of illocutionary force.

I believe that Strawson's account of (non-conventional) illocutionary force is inadequate in at least two respects. First, as suspected by Strawson, (a) fails to provide a set of jointly sufficient conditions, for each of the counter-examples in section II.1 to Grice's account of *S*-meaning (with the exception of Strawson's) is also a counter-example to (a). Secondly, it is not a necessary condition for *S* performing an illocutionary act in uttering *x* that *S* utter *x* intending to produce in a certain audience *A* a certain response *r by means of A's recognition of S's intention to produce r in A*. Consider, for instance, one of the counter-examples to Grice given in section II.3 :

> *A*: "A necessary condition of someone's meaning that *p* is that he utter a sentence which means "*p*"."
> *S*: "But then one could never mean that *p* by uttering a sentence metaphorically."

Here *S* has raised an objection to *A*'s statement (his utterance has the force of an objection), but there is no (relevant) response that *S* intends to produce in *A* by means of recognition of intention. Similar examples could be adduced to show that the condition in question is not a necessary condition for an utterance having the force of a correction, explanation, inference, or reply, to mention only some of the counter-examples to the proposed "recognition of intention" condition. Of course this condition may be a necessary condition for performing illocutionary acts of a certain kind, as, no doubt, it is a necessary condition for telling *A* that *p* or of requesting *A* to ψ.

The moral to be drawn from our brief discussion of Strawson's account of illocutionary acts which are not essentially conventional is this : the shortcomings of Strawson's account are, so to speak, also the shortcomings of Grice's account of *S*-meaning; so, for all we know, there still stands the basic idea that an account of

---

[7] The phrase 'perhaps sufficient' is used because of Strawson's fear of an infinite regression of intentions: see section II.2.

illocutionary acts can be given in terms of an account of *S*-meaning. For this reason, at least to a large extent, I should like to propose the following complex analysis of illocutionary acts.

(a) The class of kinds of illocutionary acts divides into two jointly exhaustive and mutually exclusive subclasses. Let us designate one class the "⊢" class of kinds of illocutionary acts [read: 'the assertive class . . .'], and the other the "!" class of kinds of illocutionary acts [read: 'the imperative class . . .'].

A kind of illocutionary act *I* is an ⊢ kind of illocutionary act if and only if, for any *S* and any *x*, *S* performed an act of kind *I* in uttering *x* only if, for some *p*, *S* meant that *p* by uttering *x*. Telling that, objecting, reporting, predicting, and replying are examples of ⊢ kinds of illocutionary acts.

A kind of illocutionary act *I* is an ! kind of illocutionary act if and only if, for any *S* and any *x*, *S* performed an act of kind *I* in uttering *x* only if, for some *A* and some ψ, *S* meant that *A* was to ψ by uttering *x*. Ordering, requesting, entreating, and asking are examples of ! kinds of illocutionary acts.

(The claim that the ⊢ and ! classes are mutually exclusive requires that I do not count *telling* as a kind of illocutionary act. However, telling that such-and-such is the case and telling so-and-so to do such-and-such are kinds of illocutionary acts which jointly exhaust acts of telling; so nothing is lost. A similar point is in order for suggesting, warning, etc.)

(b) The ⊢ class of kinds of illocutionary acts is in turn divisible into three jointly exhaustive and mutually exclusive subclasses of kinds of illocutionary acts, which I shall call the "*p*-identifiable" class, the "$\rho(t)$-identifiable" class, and the "*p*-and-$\rho(t)$-identifiable" class.

(1) A kind of act *I* is a *p-identifiable* kind of illocutionary act *if and only if* there is a form of beliefs *F* such that, for any *S* and any *x*, *S* performed an act of kind *I* in uttering *x* if and only if, for some *A* and some *p*, *S* uttered *x* intending it to be mutual knowledge* between him and *A* that he uttered *x* intending there to be a ρ such that his utterance of *x* causes *A* to have the activated belief that $p/\rho(t)$, etc. (i.e., *S* meant that *p* by uttering *x*), and the belief that *p* is of form *F*.

This definition requires some elucidation. Suppose that a kind of act *I* is a *p*-identifiable kind of illocutionary act. We then know that *S* performed an act of kind *I* in uttering *x* only if, for some p, S meant that p by uttering x; in other words, only if there is a proposition p such that S uttered x intending to cause A to actively believe that p, etc. We also know that the belief which S intends to activate in A must be subject to a certain sort of restriction: if in uttering x S performed a p-identifiable kind of illocutionary act, then S must have uttered x intending to activate in A a belief of a certain form (or, what for me is the same, S must have uttered x intending A actively to believe a proposition of a certain form). Admittedly, talk about the "form (I might have said 'content') of a belief (or proposition)" is not very clear *per se*, but perhaps what I have in mind will be made a bit clearer by the following condition of adequacy. A kind of act I is a p-identifiable kind of illocutionary act *only if* there is a sentence or sentence form (or sentence matrix) ϕ such that S performed an act of kind I in uttering x only if S uttered x intending to activate in A a certain belief and this belief is expressible by ϕ or a completion of ϕ. I take the notion of a sentence form (or sentence matrix) to be familiar and unproblematic.[8] And we may say that the belief that the cat is on the mat is expressible by the sentence 'The cat is on the mat' and, *a fortiori*, by a completion of the sentence form '. . . is on the mat'.

Now, for example, *answering* is a p-identifiable kind of illocutionary act: roughly, in uttering x S was answering A's question just in case S meant by uttering x that the answer to A's question was such-and-such. (This definition is not circular, despite its appearance: see below, p. 100.) So if by uttering x S meant that the answer to the question ("What time is it?") A addressed to S was that it was 6 o'clock, then in uttering x S was answering A's question.

It follows from our analysis of p-identifiable kinds of illocutionary acts that if we know that S meant that p by uttering x and if we know what S meant (the value of 'p', as it were), then we know all that we need to know in order to know what p-identifiable kinds of illocutionary acts S performed in uttering x: hence the name 'p-identifiable'. One may know that S's utterance had a certain p-identifiable kind of illocutionary force without knowing exactly what S meant, but one will at least know that S intended to activate in A a belief of such-and-such a form, and so one will at least know, as it were, the sort of thing that S meant. However, one will not know the *particular* p-identifiable

[8] See, for example, Benson Mates, *Elementary Logic*, pp. 14 and 22.

illocutionary force of *S*'s utterance *x* unless one knows what
S meant by uttering *x*. For example, if one knows that by uttering
x S meant that . . . was a reason for thinking that *A*'s statement
that . . . was false, then one knows that *S*'s utterance had the force
of an objection. But one will not know the particular illocutionary
act *S* performed in uttering *x* (i.e., the particular illocutionary
force of *S*'s utterance *x*) unless one knows that for example *S* meant
that the fact that Jones had an I.Q. of 180 was a reason for thinking that *A*'s statement that Jones was mentally retarded was false.

In addition to answering and objecting, affirming, correcting,
denying, describing, explaining, illustrating, and replying are,
I submit, further examples of *p*-identifiable kinds of illocutionary
acts. (On pp. 99–103 I offer approximate definitions of some
examples from each of the various subclasses of kinds of
illocutionary acts.)

(2) A kind of act *I* is a $\rho(t)$-*identifiable* kind of illocutionary act
if and only if there is a form of reasons (beliefs) *F* such that, for
any *S* and any *x*, *S* performed an act of kind *I* in uttering *x* if and
only if, for some *A*, *p*, and ρ, *S* uttered *x* intending it to be
mutual knowledge* between him and *A* that he uttered *x* intending to cause *A* to have the activated belief that $p/\rho(t)$, etc., and
$\rho(t)$ is of form *F*.

Whenever *S* means that *p* he must intend *A* to have *some*
reason for his belief that *p*; however, it is also true that almost
always when *S* means that *p* he intends it to be mutual knowledge*
between him and *A* that he intends *A* to have a *certain* reason for
his belief that *p*. To perform a $\rho(t)$-identifiable illocutionary act *S*
must intend *A* to have a certain truth-supporting reason for his
belief that *p*, and this reason must be of a certain form.

So if we know that *S* meant that *p* by uttering *x* and if we know
those reasons *S* intended *A* to have for his belief that *p* which are
part of the characterization of *S*'s act of meaning that *p* (i.e., if
we know the value of 'ρ', as it were), then we know all that we
need to know in order to know what $\rho(t)$-identifiable kinds of
illocutionary acts *S* performed in uttering *x*. The performance of
a $\rho(t)$-identifiable kind of illocutionary act places no restrictions
on the sort of belief *S* must intend to activate in *A*; but to know
what particular illocutionary acts of this kind *S* performed one
must know the particular value(s) of 'ρ', and this I think will
entail knowing what belief *S* intended to activate in *A* (i.e., will
entail knowing what *S* meant by uttering *x*). So, in effect, the

determination of the particular $\rho(t)$-identifiable illocutionary forces attaching to *S*'s utterance will also carry with it the determination of the particular *p*-identifiable illocutionary forces of his utterance.

I submit that to the $\rho(t)$-identifiable class of kinds of illocutionary acts belong (*inter alia*): assuring, inferring (one sense), reporting (that), suggesting (that), and telling (that).

(3) A kind of act *I* is a *p-and-$\rho(t)$-identifiable* kind of illocutionary act *if and only if* there is a form of beliefs *F* and a form of reasons (beliefs) *F'* such that, for any *S* and any *x*, *S* performed an act of kind *I* in uttering *x* if and only if, for some A, *p*, and ρ, *S* uttered *x* intending it to be mutual knowledge* between him and *A* that he uttered *x* intending to cause *A* to have the activated belief that $p/\rho(t)$, etc., and the belief that *p* is of form *F* and $p(t)$ is of form *F'*.

Thus, one will know what particular illocutionary acts of this kind *S* performed in uttering *x* just in case one knows both what *S* meant by uttering *x* (when, for some *p*, *S* meant that *p*) and the truth-supporting reasons *S* intended *A* to have for his belief that *p*. I submit that to this class belong (*inter alia*): apologizing, estimating, permitting, predicting, promising, and thanking.

(c) The ! class of kinds of illocutionary acts is analogously divisible into three jointly exhaustive and mutually exclusive subclasses, which I shall call the "ψ-identifiable" class, the "ρ-identifiable" class, and the "ψ-and-ρ-identifiable" class. The definition and remarks for each of these three class names is *mutatis mutandis* identical with the definition and remarks for the corresponding ⊢ subclass.

(1) I can think of no verb which *names* a ψ-*identifiable* kind of illocutionary act. (On p. 101 I suggest a partial explanation of why this should be the case.) Notice, however, that there is nothing to prevent us from coining a name for acts of *S* meaning that so-and-so is to ψ in which 'ψ' takes a certain sort of value, and in some languages there may actually be such verbs.[9] This raises certain obvious questions concerning the criteria for identifying *kinds* of (illocutionary) acts. I propose to avoid these problems by supposing (? pretending) that acts of a certain sort constitute a kind of illocutionary act only if there is an English verb naming that sort of act. Therefore, I will say that at present

[9] See John R. Searle, "Austin on Locutionary and Illocutionary Acts", p. 417.

the class of ψ-identifiable kinds of illocutionary acts is probably empty, although it need not remain so.

(2) Almost every ⊢ kind of illocutionary act is a *p-identifiable* kind of illocutionary act: advising, commanding, entreating, ordering, requesting, prescribing, and telling to, to name but a few of the members of this class.

(3) The only examples of *ψ-and-p-identifiable* kinds of illocutionary acts that I have been able to think of are of the interrogative sort, i.e., such speech acts as asking (whether, when, etc.), interrogating, and questioning. Perhaps this is why there is an interrogative mood.

At this point, for those who like myself enjoy visual aids, the following tree-diagram may serve as a useful summary of our hypothesis. ('*I*' designates the class of kinds of illocutionary acts.)

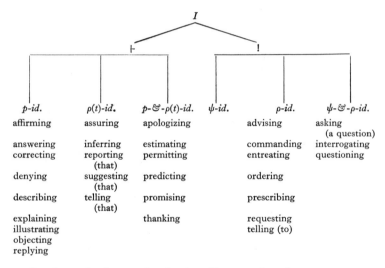

p-id.	*$\rho(t)$-id.*	*p-&-$\rho(t)$-id.*	*ψ-id.*	*ρ-id.*	*ψ-&-ρ-id.*
affirming	assuring	apologizing		advising	asking (a question)
answering	inferring	estimating		commanding	interrogating
correcting	reporting (that)	permitting		entreating	questioning
denying	suggesting (that)	predicting		ordering	
describing	telling (that)	promising		prescribing	
explaining		thanking		requesting	
illustrating				telling (to)	
objecting					
replying					

Our hypothesis may be further illustrated and to some extent confirmed by providing—as I now propose to do—approximate and not too precise definitions for some of the examples from each of the (non-empty) classes of kinds of illocutionary acts.

⊢ *Kinds of Illocutionary Acts*

(1) *p-identifiable*: objecting, explaining.

(i) In uttering *x* *S* was *objecting* to *A*'s claim (suggestion, etc.) that *q* (and objecting that *p*) *if and only if* *S* meant by uttering *x* that the fact (truth) that p constitutes a good reason for thinking that A's claim (etc.) that q is false. (If S is objecting to some act A performed (or is intending to perform), then, roughly, 'A's doing [having done] such-and-such' is to be substituted for 'A's claim that q' and 'wrong [unwise, thoughtless, etc.]' is to be substituted for 'false'.)

Now in a typical case of objecting, A says that q (e.g., A says that Mr. X is a kind and gentle man) and S tells (reminds, points out to, etc.) A that p (e.g., that Mr. X beats his wife and children), further intending A to recognize that the fact that p constitutes a good reason for thinking that A's statement that q is false. Consequently, one might doubt that the above account of objecting is correct, since it does not require that S mean that p by uttering x. However, I do not think that it is a necessary condition for objecting that p that one mean that p, despite this being what usually occurs. For it is possible for A to know that p (and to have it in mind that p) but fail to see that the fact that p is an objection to the claim that q, in which case S might simply point out to A, or perhaps even tell A, that the fact that p constitutes a good reason for thinking that A's claim that q is false, in which case, I think, S will have objected to A's claim that q.

(ii) In uttering x S was *explaining* why (what, how) . . . *if and only if* by uttering x S meant that such-and-such was why (what, how) . . .

An alternative way of analysing such speech acts as objecting, explaining, illustrating, and answering which complements the analyses given has been suggested by Grice (in conversation). Notice, to begin with, that S's utterance may have the illocutionary force of an objection (explanation, illustration, etc.), notwithstanding that in issuing his utterance S failed to produce an objection (explanation, illustration, etc.). This is possible because it may not be the case, say, that the fact that p constitutes a reason for thinking that A's claim that q is false; in other words, S may be mistaken in thinking that the fact that p is an objection to A's claim that q. This suggests that the concept of an objection (explanation, illustration, etc.) may be analysed without reference to the speech act of objecting (explaining, illustrating, etc.). For example, if one knows that p and that if p, not q, then, if one knows that so-and-so has stated that q, one is aware of an objection to so-and-so's statement that q. In a similar way one may be aware of an explanation of why . . . or of an illustration of . . . Not all of the p-identifiable kinds of illocutionary acts can be analysed in this way—there can be no affirmation without an act of affirming—but I believe that most can be so analysed. And I suspect that it is this fact which accounts for the interesting asymmetry between the ⊢ and ! classes of kinds of illocutionary acts, viz., that the ψ-identifiable class is empty.

(2) $p(t)$-*identifiable*: telling (that), reporting (that), assuring.

(i) In uttering x S was *telling* A that p *if and only if* by uttering x S meant that p and S intended it to be mutual knowledge* between him and A that he intended part of A's reason for believing that p to be that S uttered x intending A to think that S believed (he knew) that p.

(ii) In uttering x S was *reporting* that p *if and only if* by uttering x S meant that p and S intended it to be mutual knowledge* between him and A that he intended part of A's reason for believing that p to be that S uttered x intending A to think that, on the basis of S's observations (or investigations), S believed (he knew) that p.

Acts of reporting are a subclass of acts of telling. When S reports that p he not only intends to make known to A that he thinks that p, he also intends to make known, to some extent, *why* he thinks that p. The rationale for this is patent: whether or not A takes the fact that S believes (he knows) that p as evidence that p may well depend on A's belief as to how S arrived at his belief that p.

(iii) In uttering x S was *assuring* A that p *if and only if* by uttering x S meant that p and S intended it to be mutual knowledge* between him and A that he intended part of A's reason for believing that p to be that S uttered x intending A to think that S is justifiably certain that p.

Acts of assuring are also a subclass of acts of telling. The rationale for the additional feature here is again patent: knowledge of how firmly S holds his belief that p is certainly relevant information in determining whether to think that p on the basis of thinking that S thinks that p.

(3) p-and-$p(t)$-*identifiable*: estimating, thanking.

(i) In uttering x S was *estimating* that the value (cost, number, size, etc.) of so-and-so was such-and-such *if and only if* by uttering x S meant that the value (etc.) of so-and-so was approximately such-and-such and S intended it to be mutual knowledge* between him and A that he intended part of A's reason for believing that the value (etc.) of so-and-so was approximately such-and-such to be that *S* uttered *x* intending *A* to think that, as a result of having examined so-and-so and of having applied to his findings certain general knowledge of his concerning the value (etc.) of things of the type to which so-and-so belongs, *S* believed (he knew) that the value (etc.) of so-and-so was approximately such-and-such.

(ii) In uttering *x S* was *thanking* [primary sense] *A* for doing such-and-such *if and only if* in uttering *x S* was telling *A* that *S* was grateful to *A* for doing such-and-such (or appreciative of *A*'s doing such-and-such).

In England it is customary for a waiter in certain sorts of restaurants to "thank" (say 'Thank you.' to) the person he is serving when serving that person, presumably for the privilege of serving him. In such a case, it seems to me, the waiter does *not* mean that he is appreciative of the privilege of serving one. Nor do I think that there is anything else that the waiter means by uttering 'Thank you'. Moreover, I think that (1) such cases are cases of thanking only in a "secondary" or "inverted commas" sense of 'thank', and so are not counter-examples to the above definition; (2) in such cases the waiter is not performing an illocutionary act; and (3) points of the same sort as the preceding two are applicable to most of the speech acts Austin called "behabitives". There are, I submit, *social* conventions requiring certain sorts of people in certain sorts of circumstances to *go through the motions* of thanking (by saying 'Thank you.'), or of apologizing (by saying 'I apologize.'), or of congratulating (by saying 'I congratulate you.'), etc., and it is this fact which accounts for the secondary uses of these terms (cf. section III.3).

! Kinds of Illocutionary Acts

(1) *p-identifiable* : ordering, advising.

(i) In uttering *x S* was *ordering A* to *ψ if and only if* by uttering *x S* meant that *A* was to *ψ* and *S* intended it to be mutual knowledge* between him and *A* that he intended part of *A*'s reason for *ψ*-ing to be : that there was a certain legal or conventional or institutional relation *R* between *S* and *A* such that by virtue of their being related in way *R S* had the right to expect *A* to do an act of such-and-such a sort if in circumstances of such-and-such a sort *S* means that *A* is to do a certain act of that sort; that *ψ* was an act of the relevant sort; and that the circumstances in which S uttered x were of the relevant sort.

(ii) In uttering x S was *advising* A to ψ *if and only if* by uttering x S meant that A **was** to (should) ψ and S intended it to be mutual knowledge* between him and A that he intended part of A's reason for ψ-ing to be that it was in A's best interest to ψ.

(2) *ψ-and-ρ-identifiable*. I have already suggested (in section III.5) that to ask a question is to request information. Thus, for example, S asked A when . . . just in case S requested A to inform him, S, of when . . . I am not entirely confident that interrogating is a kind of illocutionary act, but I think that a case could be made for thinking that it belongs to this class of kinds of illocutionary acts and that the difference between interrogating and asking (a question) lies in the different restrictions each kind of act imposes on the kind of reason S must intend A to have for providing S with the information desired by S.

A few concluding remarks.

(1) It follows from our hypothesis that a kind of act I is a kind of illocutionary act if and only if I is a p-identifiable, a $\rho(t)$-identifiable, a p-and-$\rho(t)$-identifiable, a ψ-identifiable, a ρ-identifiable or a ψ-and-ρ-identifiable kind of illocutionary act; and it further follows that S performed an illocutionary act in uttering x if and only if S performed an act of any one of these kinds. Therefore, S performed an illocutionary act in uttering x *only if* S meant something by uttering x. But it does not *follow* that S performed an illocutionary act in uttering x *if* S meant something by uttering x. Doubtless, however, there are enough kinds of illocutionary acts to secure that S performed an illocutionary act in uttering x if and only if S meant something by uttering x.

(2) It is worth remarking that Austin's notion of uptake—the bringing about in one's audience of the understanding of the meaning and of the force of one's utterance—is easily recoverable on the above account of illocutionary force: S secured uptake of his utterance x if and only if S meant something by uttering x and the mutual knowledge* (belief*) which S must intend to secure if he is to mean something by uttering x was secured by

S by uttering *x*. This definition anticipates some of the results of section IV.4.

(3) There are certain kinds of speech acts, classed by Austin as kinds of illocutionary acts, which are such that a necessary condition for the performance of a speech act of any one of these kinds is that one utter a sentence having a certain sort of meaning. I have especially in mind the speech act of stating (asserting); for, roughly speaking, a necessary condition for stating (asserting) that *p* is that one utter a sentence which means "*p*". So it may seem that I should allow for a class of "*x*-identifiable" kinds of illocutionary acts. Nevertheless, I propose to go along with Austin's distinction between illocutionary acts and acts of saying (at least to some extent) but to treat stating (asserting), unlike Austin, as one kind of act of saying.

(4) There may well be other speech acts which Austin would call illocutionary acts but which do not fit neatly or precisely or at all into the above schema. I do not take this to be an objection to my account of illocutionary force. For I should like the proffered account of illocutionary force to be taken as an attempt to provide a theoretical explanation and, *a fortiori*, a justification of Austin's insight that (at least many of) the acts he classed as illocutionary acts do share a set of features by virtue of which an understanding of such acts is necessary for an understanding of language and communication.

IV.3 *Explicit performatives*

Since "On Denoting" it has not been uncommon for philosophers to argue in the following way. A certain type of utterance has the grammatical appearance of having a certain logical form, but the grammatical form of utterances of this type is misleading, for they have a different logical form from the one they appear to have. It was Austin's belief that with his discovery of explicit performative utterances he had unmasked a hitherto unnoticed class of 'masqueraders", a class of utterances having a logical form quite different from the one their grammatical form would lead one to think they have. But there is a very important difference between Austin's purported discovery and the usual claims concomitant with such unmaskings. Usually what is argued is that utterances of such-and-such a type (e.g., utterances of the form '. . . is wrong'), which appear to be of one standard and familiar logical form (e.g., they appear to be "true or false statements"), are really of a different standard and familiar logical form (e.g., they are really "imperatives"). Austin, however, does not attempt to reduce explicit performatives to some antecedently familiar logical form. If what Austin says about explicit performatives is correct, he will have discovered *a new logical form* (or forms—depending upon how one views the matter). This is why Austin's thesis about explicit performatives is so important, if correct. An argument to show that it is not correct might enhance the hypothesis put forward in the preceding section.

An explicit performative sentence is a sentence beginning with a verb in the first person singular present indicative active, this verb being the name of the kind of (illocutionary) act one would (ordinarily) be performing in uttering that sentence. For example, 'I (hereby) order you to leave', 'I (hereby) promise to pay you twopence', and 'I (hereby) warn you that there's a snake in your bed' are explicit performative sentences (the parenthetical 'hereby' precludes these sentences from being uttered to make statements about how one habitually behaves or about the historic present). Such utterances *appear grammatically* to be of the sort used to make true or false statements—in this case, statements to the effect that the speaker is at the moment of issuing the utterance performing an act of the sort named by the verb in the first person singular present indicative active. To use Austin's term for sentences used in the making of statements, explicit performative sentences appear to be "constative" in logical form. Using the Fregean device of assertion sign plus sentence radical, we may say that, e.g., 'I (hereby) promise to pay you twopence', has the appearance of being of the form

⊢ [my (hereby) promising to pay you twopence].

But, Austin claims, explicit performatives are not constative. Such utterances are neither true nor false. In uttering an explicit performative, e.g., 'I (hereby) order you to leave', one does not mean that one is ordering *A* to leave; one is not saying (stating, asserting, reporting, telling) that one is ordering *A* to leave. Austin does not argue for this claim; in fact, he thinks this point so obvious that it needs no argument.[10] In uttering an explicit performative sentence one does not mean that one is performing an act of the sort named by the explicit performative verb; rather, in uttering an explicit performative sentence one is

[10] *How to Do Things with Words*, p. 6.

performing an act of the sort named by the explicit performative verb. The job of the explicit performative formula is that of "*making explicit* (which is not the same as stating or describing) what precise action it is that is being performed by the issuing of the utterance" (ibid., p. 61); and, *a fortiori*, the explicit performative formula is a device used for performing acts of the kind named by the explicit performative verb. We might express this last point by saying that the way to represent an explicit performative, such as 'I (hereby) promise to pay you twopence', is not

⊢ [my (hereby) promising to pay you twopence],

but rather

Pr [my paying you twopence],

where '*Pr*' is to be taken as a conventional force-indicating device which makes explicit that an utterance of the sentence has the force of a promise, just as '⊢' would serve to make explicit that an assertion is being made.[11]

Why did Austin think that explicit performative utterances are not constative?

(1) Austin sometimes gives the impression of thinking that the fact that in uttering an explicit performative sentence one is performing an act of the kind named by the explicit performative verb is incompatible with one's also stating that one is performing such an act.

(2) A better argument is perhaps the following one, which may have been behind Austin's claim, if only implicitly.

(i) Ordinarily, explicit performative sentences (like all or most other sentences) are uttered with their full conventional force or meaning.

(ii) Therefore, if explicit performatives have the conventional force of being constative, then, ordinarily, in uttering an explicit performative one is constating that one is performing an act of the kind named by the explicit performative verb.

(iii) If the consequent of (ii) were true, then, ordinarily, it would be true to say of someone who uttered an explicit performative—say, 'I (hereby) order you to leave'—that he said or meant or stated that he was ordering *A* to leave.

(iv) But it would not be true to say of someone who uttered,

<hr>

[11] Cf. Searle, *Speech Acts*, especially Chapter II.

say, 'I (hereby) order you to leave' that he said (etc.) that he was ordering *A* to leave.

(v) Therefore, explicit performative sentences are not constative.

I agree with Austin that in uttering an explicit performative one is not constating that one is performing an act of the kind named by the explicit performative verb, and I agree with him that ordinarily one uses the explicit performative formula to make explicit the precise act one is performing in the issuing of one's utterance. But I wish to deny that explicit performative sentences are not constative. That is, I wish to assert that there is no difference of the sort claimed in logical form or conventional force between, say, 'I (hereby) order you to leave' and 'I am scratching my head' or 'The cat is on the mat'. For I will also deny that explicit performatives are uttered with their full conventional force or meaning (i.e., I deny (i) and, *a fortiori*, (ii) of the above argument). So if I am right, Austin is wrong in his claim to have exposed a new class of masqueraders.

First I will argue that explicit performatives are constative. Then I will argue that even though they are constative in logical form, explicit performatives are not uttered with their full conventional force; that is, I will argue that in uttering, say, 'I order you to leave' *S* does not mean thereby (is not constating) that he is ordering *A* to leave.

(a) It was argued in section III.2 that, since to tell someone that *p* is (roughly) to utter something with the primary intention of informing him, by means of recognition of intention, that *p*, then, presumably,

σ_1: I (hereby) tell you that *p*

means roughly the same as

σ_2: My primary intention in uttering this sentence is to inform you, by means of recognition of intention, that *p*.

So if it is to be argued that explicit performatives are not constative, then it must be argued either that (1) σ_2 is not constative, or that (2) explicit performative verbs (in this case 'tell') undergo a change of meaning when they occur in the first person singular present indicative active (at least in certain constructions).

That (1) should be the case seems most implausible. It would be tantamount to the claim that σ_2 and 'A primary intention of mine in uttering this sentence is to annoy you' are of relevantly different logical forms. Surely anyone who uttered either of these sentences would intend his utterance to make known his intentions by virtue of his audience's knowledge of the meaning of the words, the word order, and the fact that the sentence uttered is in the indicative mood.

But (2) seems equally implausible. First, it is not at all clear what would be meant by the claim that 'tell' "undergoes a change of meaning" (at least sometimes) when it occurs in the first person singular present indicative active. Certainly it is not that 'tell' has a different *paraphrase* when it occurs as an explicit performative. Nor should we want, I think, to claim that 'tell' differs in meaning in the sentences

I (am) tell(ing) you that *p*

and

If I (am) tell(ing) you that *p*, then *q*.

Secondly, given that the point of using the explicit performative formula is to make explicit what illocutionary act one is performing, this job can be done quite well on the assumption that the explicit performative sentence is an ordinary indicative (constative) sentence. For if to perform a certain illocutionary act is just to utter something with certain intentions, then if, as it were, one says that one is issuing one's utterance with those intentions and if, as it were, one is speaking truthfully, then one will be performing that illocutionary act in issuing the utterance. So if explicit performative verbs undergo a change of "meaning", they undergo that change only to perform the same job they would perform had they not undergone that change!

(b) Nevertheless, I do not believe that, ordinarily, in uttering an explicit performative one is constating that one is performing a certain illocutionary act. In the first place, our intuitions count for something, and I believe Austin was correct at least in claiming that one who says, e.g., 'I (hereby) order you to leave' would not be *said* to have *asserted that* he was ordering *A* to leave. Secondly, if it were true that in uttering, e.g., 'I (hereby) order you to leave' one was asserting that one was ordering *A* to leave, then it would not be possible for one to make explicit by the explicit performative device the *full* illocutionary force of one's utterance. For suppose *S* says 'I (hereby) order you to leave' and that in saying this *S*—in addition to ordering *A* to leave—is asserting that he is ordering *A* to leave. Were *S* to have made explicit the full illocutionary force of his utterance, then, he would have to have at least said

I (hereby) assert that I (hereby) order you to leave.

But had he uttered this, *S* would have been asserting that he was asserting that he was ordering *A* to leave, and so he would still not have been making explicit the full illocutionary force of his utterance. And so on, *ad infinitum*. Yet one can make explicit by the explicit performative device the full illocutionary force of one's utterance. One who says 'I (hereby) order you to leave' is *not* asserting (constating) that he is ordering *A* to leave.

We can explain why it should be the case that in uttering an explicit performative sentence one does not mean that one is performing a certain illocutionary act, despite the fact that explicit performative sentences are constative in logical form.

The view that I wish to subscribe to is as follows. Think of an explicit performative sentence, say, 'I (hereby) order you to leave' as being representable as

⊢ [my (hereby) ordering you to leave],

where '⊢' is a conventional means—roughly corresponding, to some extent, to the indicative mood in English—for making known to an audience that one's primary intention in uttering '⊢[. . .]' is to produce (or activate) in one's audience a certain belief, the content of which is specified by what appears within the brackets. We may call this a standard conventional implication of '⊢'. It follows, then, that if one were to utter an explicit performative with its full standard conventional force, one would mean that one was performing such-and-such illocutionary act. But I suggest that when one utters an explicit performative sentence one utters that sentence with something slightly less than that sentence's full conventional force. One utters an explicit performative sentence, say, 'I (hereby) order you to leave' ('⊢ [my (hereby) ordering you to leave]') with something slightly less than its full conventional force, for when one utters 'I (hereby) order you to leave' one intends it to be mutual knowledge* between oneself and one's audience *A* that one's primary intention is to get *A* to leave (and not to produce in *A* the belief that one is ordering *A* to leave). That the explicit performative sentence is being uttered with something slightly less than its full conventional force (as it were, with something slightly less than the full standard conventional implication of '⊢') is made known by a combination of things; these are predominantly: the meaning of the sentence uttered (as it were, the propositional content '[my (hereby) ordering you to leave]' cancels out part of the standard conventional implication of '⊢') and the reason a speaker is likely to have for uttering such a sentence, viz., to make explicit the illocutionary force of his utterance. Otherwise, the way in which an explicit performative sentence makes known one's intentions is in principle no different from the way in which 'I intend to go to the cinema' would make known one's intention to go to the cinema.

IV.4 *Saying and locutionary acts*

Let us round off our discussion of speech acts by (a) defining the second of the two senses distinguished in section I.1 in which a person may be said to have meant something; by (b) saying what it is for someone to say something; and by (c) saying a few things about Austin's notion of the locutionary act.

(a) *S meant ". . ." by x*.

In the informal discussion of the meanings of 'meaning' in Chapter I, I said that utterances of the form

S meant ". . ." by *x*

are used to report the sense or meaning *S* intended *x* to have on the occasion of his uttering *x* and that, accordingly, the value of '*x*' may be a word, a phrase, or a sentence. A more precise definition is now due; but first a notational convenience should be adopted. Let '*Σ*' stand for any complete utterance, and read '*Σ(x)*' as '*Σ* containing *x*'. It will be understood that every utterance contains itself, so that *x* may be identical with *Σ*.

> When *S* uttered *Σ(x)*, *S* meant ". . ." by *x* iff *S* uttered *Σ(x)* intending thereby to realize a certain state of affairs *E* which is (intended by *S* to be) such that *E* includes the fact that *x* means (timeless) ". . ." and such that the obtainment of *E* is sufficient for *S* and a certain audience *A* mutually knowing* (or believing*) that *E* obtains and that *E* is conclusive (very good or good) evidence that

(1) *S* uttered *x* because *x* means (timeless) ". . ." [more precisely: it is a necessary part of a sufficient—but not necessarily necessary—reason of *S*'s for uttering *x* that *x* means (timeless) ". . ."];

(2) *S* uttered *Σ*(*x*) intending to realize *E*.

Our primary interest in wanting to know what *S* meant by *x* is to enable us to determine what he meant by uttering *Σ*(*x*). Nevertheless, we noticed in Chapter I that *S* may mean "*p*" by *Σ*, and may mean something by (or in) uttering *Σ*, but not mean that *p* by uttering *Σ*. The example I used there was a case where *S* uttered 'I'm in hock' and meant by 'I'm in hock', "I'm in debt", but meant by uttering 'I'm in hock' that he was in excellent financial shape. We also noticed that *S* may mean something by *Σ*, yet not mean anything by uttering *Σ*. Both of these possibilities are preserved by our definition.

Notice, too, that in order for *S* to mean ". . ." by *x*, *S* must think that *x* means ". . .". (This does not rule out the case where *x* means [timeless] ". . ." as a result of a transient convention, such as a password or code.) There are certain apparent counter-examples to this feature of our definition, but I believe that they are not actual counter-examples. For example, *S* may utter 'Richard is a lion' and mean thereby that Richard is brave. In such a case one might be inclined to say that *S* meant "brave" by 'lion'. However, I should want to say that one who said this would either be speaking incorrectly or speaking elliptically, as it were, in which case one would mean, roughly, that by uttering '. . . lion' *S* meant that . . . brave.

Finally, we should also want to be able to say that *S* may mean something by *x* even though there is no intended audience. Let us stipulate that in the limiting case, *S* = *A*.

(b) *Saying*

There are at least two senses of 'say' in which a person may be truly said to have said something.

The least interesting case is the use of 'say' in contexts of *direct quotation*. (Hereinafter, I shall write 'say$_d$' for this sense of 'say'.) When we report what someone said$_d$, we report the words he actually uttered, whether or not he meant anything by them and whether or not he meant anything by uttering them. Accordingly:

S said$_d$ something iff there was a word or phrase or sentence *x* and a language *L* such that *x* belonged to *L* and *x* was uttered by *S* as belonging to *L*.

S said$_d$ *x* iff *x* was a word or phrase or sentence belonging to a language *L* and *x* was uttered by *S* as belonging to *L*.

(This sense of 'say', which Austin suggests is an "inverted commas" sense, corresponds to Austin's phatic act.)[12] This analysis is intended to encompass both spoken and written utterances. If this bothers anyone, the analysandum may be altered to read '*S* said$_d$ or wrote$_d$ . . .'. A similar qualification will be in order for our next definition.

The most interesting sense of 'say' is the use of 'say' in contexts of *indirect quotation*, as exemplified in

S said that the cat was on the mat

and in

S said that you were to leave.

(Hereinafter I shall write 'say$_i$' for this sense of 'say'.)

A familiar problem arises when we attempt to say what it is for *S* to say$_i$ something; so I shall proceed in the same sort of way as I did in giving an account of *S*-meaning, and first seek an analysis of what it is for *S* to say$_i$ that *p*. Here is a first approximation:

S said$_i$ that *p* iff there was a sentence σ such that when *S* uttered σ *S* both meant "*p*" by σ and meant that *p* by uttering σ.

I do not think this account is quite adequate as it stands. For suppose that *S* utters 'He is a conservative' and means thereby that the President of the U.S.A. in 1972 is a conservative. In such an event it would be true to say that *S* said$_i$ that the President of the U.S.A. in 1972 was a conservative; but it would not be true to say that by 'he' *S* meant "the President of the U.S.A. in 1972." (It could perhaps be said that by 'he' *S* meant the President of the U.S.A. in 1972. This is what might be said in response to the question "*Whom* did you mean by 'he'?" But here 'mean' has the force of 'refer to', and the expression occurring to the right of the verb 'mean' would not be placed (by me) within double

---

[12] *How to Do Things with Words*, pp. 95–6.

quotation marks. At any rate, it is clear that if my account of what it is for S to mean something by x is correct, then it would not be true that by 'he' S meant "the President . . .") The problem that arises with regard to 'he' is, of course, a problem that arises with regard to any "indicator" word—that is, such words as 'he', 'she', 'I', 'you', 'it', 'there', 'here', 'now', 'today', etc. It is necessary, then, to say something about indicator words before our analysis of saying$_i$ can be revised.

Consider the two sentences

σ_1: Grass is green

and

σ_2: It is green.

To know the meaning of σ_1 is to know what a speaker of English would (ordinarily) mean were he to utter σ_1. This is not true of σ_2: if we know that S uttered σ_2 with its full conventional force, then we know that there was something x (or so S believed) such that S intended A to think x was green. But without further information about the physical and/or linguistic context in which the sentence was uttered we will not know what S intended A to think was green, and, *a fortiori*, we will not know what S meant by uttering σ_2. But one cannot utter σ_2 with its full conventional force without meaning that so-and-so is green. For, quite roughly speaking, to know the meaning of an indicator word n is to know a rule or set of rules such that on the assumption that $\Sigma(n)$ was issued with its full conventional force (and assuming one knows the meanings of the other words contained in Σ, etc.), one will be able to determine (or to some extent to determine) by the application of these rules to the particular circumstances of the issuing of $\Sigma(n)$ what S meant by uttering $\Sigma(n)$.

Let us say that what S meant by uttering a sentence σ was *M-compatible* with what S meant by σ just in case what S meant by uttering σ was a result of uttering σ with its full conventional force with respect to that sense of σ which S meant by σ.

A few elucidatory comments are needed before this notion of *M*-compatibility can be used in an account of saying$_i$. (1) The sentence 'Grass is green.' is a conventional means for a speaker's meaning that grass is green. Therefore, the sentence 'Grass is green.' will be uttered with its full conventional force only if by uttering this sentence one means that grass is green. But *S*'s meaning that the President of the U.S.A. in 1972 is a conservative may also be a result of uttering 'He's a conservative.' with that sentence's full conventional force. This will be so if the conventions governing the use of 'he' are such that *S* uttered 'He . . .' in accordance with those conventions and meant thereby that the President of the U.S.A. in 1972 . . . (2) The sentence 'He owns a cape.' has two meanings: "he owns a short sleeveless cloak" and "he owns a promontory of land". So it is a good idea to talk about the full conventional force of a sentence with respect to a certain sense or meaning of that sentence. To talk about what *S* meant by σ is, I have suggested, to talk about the sense or meaning of σ which *S* intended σ to have on the occasion of his uttering σ. Now ". . ." is a sense (meaning) of σ which *S* meant by σ just in case σ means ". . ." and *S* meant ". . ." by σ.

After all this I submit that

> *S* said$_i$ that *p* iff there was a sentence σ such that: that *S* meant that *p* by uttering σ, and what *S* meant by uttering σ was *M*-compatible with what *S* meant by σ.

(I should like to add that, as far as my intuitions go, in uttering σ *S* stated (asserted) that *p* just in case in uttering σ *S* said$_i$ that *p*.) Similarly:

> *S* said$_i$ that so-and-so was to ψ iff there was a sentence σ such that *S* meant that so-and-so was to ψ by uttering σ, and what *S* meant by uttering σ was *M*-compatible with what *S* meant by σ.

I further submit that

> *S* said$_i$ something iff for some *p* and some ψ, *S* said$_i$ that *p* or *S* said$_i$ that so-and-so was to ψ.

Notice that it is a consequence of this account of what it is to say$_i$ something that if *S* utters

> What time is it?

he will not have said$_i$ anything, unless it was that *A* was to inform him of the time. I do not consider this result objectionable. For if *S* said$_i$ something, then there will be some true sentence of the form

> *S* said$_i$ . . .

which specifies *what* S said$_t$. But if S utters 'What time is it?', there is no way of completing 'S said$_i$ . . .'; or at least no way of completing this sentence form which indicates that S uttered a sentence in the interrogative mood. So far as I know this fact is not peculiar to the English language.

Now if S utters 'What time is it?' and someone asks what S said$_i$, it may be replied that S *asked* what the time was. It may be objected, then, that in the case of interrogative utterances we may report what S said$_i$ by saying what he asked. (This seems to be the line taken by Austin.) But in order to take this position it would have to be maintained, I think, that (1) 'S asked . . .' entailed 'S said$_i$ . . .', which we have seen not to be the case, or else that (2) 'say$_i$' and 'ask' are cognates of the same verb. (I do not think that anyone would wish to maintain (2), but an objection will be given to it shortly.) Or *at least* it would have to be maintained that one could invent a verb and provide an unequivocal and non-disjunctive definition for it which would cover (and only cover) both cases of saying$_i$ and asking (a question). Yet there would seem to be a decisive objection to such a suggestion: necessarily, if S said$_i$ something, then S uttered a token of a whole-utterance type which means (timeless) something; but it is possible for one to ask what the time is without uttering a token of a type which has meaning. For instance, a foreigner might ask what the time is by performing some non-conventional gesture.

I believe there is a reason (or the suggestion of a reason) why saying$_i$ is especially tied to the indicative and imperative moods but not to the interrogative mood—a reason which reflects the semantical and grammatical resemblances between the relevant senses of 'say' and 'mean'. Consider the following three sentences.

σ_1: The cat is on the mat.
σ_2: Put the cat on the mat!
σ_3: Is the cat on the mat?

To know the meaning of σ_1, is just to know that it is a conventional means for meaning that the cat is on the mat. To know the meaning of σ_2 is just to know that it is a conventional means for meaning that so-and-so is to put the cat on the mat. Neither sentences in the indicative mood nor sentences in the imperative mood require as part of their conventional force that someone uttering a sentence of that sort be performing an illocutionary act of any particular kind. (This last statement requires slight qualification: sometimes the content of an indicative sentence will necessitate that one uttering that sentence with its full conventional force be performing a certain *p*-identifiable kind of illocutionary act, but that is beside the main point.) On the other hand, one will not understand the meaning of σ_3 unless one knows that it is a conventional means for *asking* whether the cat is on the mat.

(c) *Locutionary acts*

Let us recall Austin's suggestion that the locutionary act *S* performed when he uttered a sentence σ is to be identified both with *S*'s act of saying$_i$ what he said$_i$ when he uttered σ and *S*'s act of meaning what he meant by σ. If what I have said about what it is to say$_i$ something and about what it is to mean something by σ is even approximately correct, then Austin cannot correctly identify the locutionary act with both of these acts.

There is, I think, an explanation of why Austin may have thought that *S*'s act of saying$_i$ something in (when) uttering σ is the same act as *S*'s act of meaning something by σ. In his examination of the total speech act in the total speech situation Austin expressly restricts himself to those cases where an utterance is used in its "full normal use". Using a characterization of Searle's,[13] we may say that Austin restricts himself to those cases where an utterance (sentence) is "seriously and literally" uttered. Let us say that a sentence σ is seriously uttered just in case *S* meant something by uttering σ; and let us say that σ is literally uttered just in case what *S* meant by uttering σ is *M*-compatible with what *S* meant by σ. Now if one conflates what it is to mean something by σ with what it is to mean something by a serious literal utterance of σ (or what it is to mean something by σ when one seriously and literally utters σ), then, indeed, it may seem that *S* meant something by σ just in case *S* said$_i$ something in uttering σ; for, e.g., *S* meant something by 'The cat is on the mat.' when he seriously and literally uttered 'The cat is on the mat.' just in case *S* said$_i$ that the cat was on the mat when he uttered 'The cat is on the mat.'. But *S* may mean something by σ even though he did not seriously utter σ (he may have been telling a joke) and even though he did not utter σ literally (he may have been speaking ironically or metaphorically).

---

[13] "Austin on Locutionary and Illocutionary Acts", p. 406.

I suggest that if we amend Austin slightly and hold that *S* performed a locutionary act when he uttered σ if and only if *S* meant something by σ, then we shall have an account of locutionary acts which is clear, in accord with Austin's general theory, and immune to the objections brought against the locutionary/illocutionary act distinction by L. J. Cohen and by Searle.[14]

[14] L. J. Cohen, "Do Illocutionary Forces Exist?"; Searle, "Austin on Locutionary and Illocutionary Acts".

V

UTTERANCE-MEANING AND CONVENTION

Introduction

IN Chapter I, I suggested that the class of things which both mean something and have meaning subdivides into four subclasses: the class of whole-utterance types, the class of whole-utterance tokens, the class of part-utterance types, and the class of part-utterance tokens. I also argued there that the concept of a whole-utterance type is logically prior to the concept of a part-utterance type. Since whole- and part-utterance tokens can be easily and directly defined in terms of whole- and part-utterance types, the order of logical priorities is the same as the order in which these four classes are listed. Therefore, in providing an account of utterance-meaning, we should first seek to provide an account of whole-utterance types.

In Chapter I we also noticed that the class of whole-utterance types subdivides into the class of *composite* whole-utterance types and the class of *non-composite* whole-utterance types. A whole-utterance type x is a *non-composite* whole-utterance type just in case there is no "proper part" of x, y, such that both y means something and the meaning of x is determined in part by the meaning of y. In this chapter (section V.1) I offer an account of non-composite whole-utterance types, leaving composite whole-utterance types and language and some remarks about part-utterance types for the next and final chapter. There are two reasons for taking on non-composite whole-utterance types before composite whole-utterance types: first, it is generally both easier and more illuminating to move from the simple to the complex, and secondly, non-composite whole-utterance types are historically or evolutionarily prior to composite whole-utterance types. It is a fair assumption that our remote ancestors communicated by unstructured grunts and gestures before they discovered the utility of language.

That x means something in a group G is a matter of convention. Accordingly, the account of utterance-meaning I offer will be strengthened and confirmed if it can be shown to fall within an account of convention in general. Such an account is put forward in sections V.2 and V.3.

V.1. *Non-composite whole-utterance types*

Let us begin by seeking an answer to the question: What is it for *x* to be a non-composite whole-utterance type which means (timeless) "*p*" in a group *G*? (Hereinafter, for short, '*x* (*nc*) means "*p*" in *G*'.)

Suppose that in a certain community a certain type of sound (*nc*) means "there's a rabbit hunt today". It is clear that it is not solely in virtue of any of its physical or observable features that this sound has the meaning it has. No one could tell by simply hearing the sound that it has meaning. In another community the same type of sound may mean something entirely different or nothing at all.

It is reasonable to think that whether *x* (*nc*) means something in a group *G* will depend upon what members of *G* do with *x*, how they use *x*. In particular, it is reasonable to think that there is an intimate connection between what *x* (*nc*) means in *G* and what members of *G* do, would, or could mean by uttering *x*. Surely it is no accident that people mean that *p* by uttering *x* if *x* (*nc*) means "*p*". At the minimum we should expect that *x* (*nc*) means "p" in *G* only if members of *G* are able to mean that *p* by uttering *x* in certain sorts of circumstances.

While this modest condition is doubtless a necessary condition, it is not a sufficient condition for *x* (*nc*) meaning "*p*" in *G*. For suppose that it is mutual knowledge* amongst the members of *G* that the utterance-type 'grrr' resembles the sound dogs make when they are angry. A consequence of this might be that in appropriate circumstances any members of *G*, *S*, could utter 'grrr' intending that some other member of *G*, infer, at least in part on the basis of its being mutual knowledge* between him and *S* that 'grrr' resembles the sound dogs make when they are angry, that *S*'s intention in uttering 'grrr' was to communicate thereby that *S* was angry. But on the basis of this possibility alone it would not be correct to say that 'grrr' means "I am angry" in *G*. Nor would it do simply to amend the story by supposing that members of *G* frequently or always communicate that they are angry by uttering 'grrr', for we could still conceive of its being the case that on each occasion that a member of G means that he is angry by uttering 'grrr', he intends the relevant feature f of 'grrr' (from which the audience is to a large extent expected to infer that by uttering 'grrr' the utterer meant that he was angry) to be the fact that 'grrr' resembles the sound dogs make when they are angry. No doubt such a state of affairs could exist—for reasons to be made clear shortly—only in very special circumstances, but it is not inconceivable, and if this were the case it would be false that 'grrr' (nc) means "I am angry" in G.

What precludes 'grrr' from meaning "I am angry" in the above sketch, despite its being an effective means for communicating that one is angry, is that the relevant feature f—'grrr' resembling the sound dogs make when they are angry—in virtue of which (in part) an utterance of 'grrr' would be evidence that the utterer meant thereby that he was angry, is a "natural" feature, and so 'grrr', though a means for communicating that one is angry, is a non-conventional means for communicating that one is angry. What we want to find is the difference between x being a non-conventional means for communicating that p and x being a conventional means for communicating that p.

If x is such that any member of G could communicate that p to any other member of G by uttering x, then, on the basis of the proposed account of S-meaning, one should expect that there is some one special feature (or set of related features) f of x such that it is mutual knowledge* amongst the members of G that x is f, and the 'grrr' example suggests that if x is to (nc) mean "p" in G, then the relevant feature f of x must be of a certain type. Specifically, the above discussion suggests that this feature f must not be one that is true of x independently of people meaning something by uttering x. And this gives us reason to suppose that x (nc) means "p" in G only if members of G are able to mean that p by uttering x as a result of its being mutual knowledge* amongst the members of G that members of G have meant or mean or have agreed to mean that p by uttering x. In other words, there is a prima facie plausibility in thinking that x (nc) means "p" in G only if the relevant feature f of x is the fact that members of G have meant or do mean that p by uttering x. In what follows I should like to make this plausibility at least slightly more than prima facie.

x might mean nothing in G at one time and (nc) mean "p" in G at some later time. A sketch of one "possible" way this might come about will not only be helpful in arriving at an account of what it is for *x* to (*nc*) mean "*p*" in *G*, it will also serve to indicate how our account of *S*-meaning suggests an explanation of the essential facts about utterance-meaning in terms of a general account of rational goal-directed behaviour.

Before offering such a sketch it will be useful to have the following points in mind.

1. If a (rational) person *S* desires to bring about a certain result *e*, *S* will, *ceteris paribus*, choose that means (do that act) which he thinks is the surest means available in the circumstances for bringing about *e*. In other words, if *S* desires to bring about *e* and if the (subjective) probability that *e* will obtain on the assumption that *S* does *x* is greater than the (subjective) probability that *e* will obtain on the assumption that he does any other available act *y*, then, *ceteris paribus*, *S* will do *x*.

2. Suppose that *S* wants to communicate to *A* that *p*. *S* will utter *x* only if he thinks that *A* will (or might) think—on the basis of thinking that *S* uttered *x* in the circumstances—that *S* meant that *p* by uttering *x*. That is, *S* will utter *x* only if *S* thinks that *A* will (or might) believe that an utterance of *x* by *S* in the circumstances is evidence that *S* meant that *p* by uttering *x*. Now, uttering *x* in circumstances *C* is (for *S*) a surer means of communicating to *A* that *p* than is uttering *y* in *C* if *A* thinks that the evidence provided by an utterance of *x* by *S* in *C* for its being the case that *S* meant that *p* by uttering *x* is better than the evidence provided by an utterance of *y* by *S* in *C* for its being the case that *S* meant that *p* by uttering *y*. In other words, the more likely it is that *A* will infer from the fact that *S* uttered *x* in circumstances *C* that *S* meant thereby that *p*, the surer *x* is as a means for communicating to *A* that *p* in circumstances *C*.

Therefore, if *S* wants to communicate to *A* that *p* and if *S* thinks that *A* will think that an utterance of *x* by *S* in the circumstances is evidence that *S* meant that *p* and if *S* thinks that there is no other available utterance-type *y*, such that *A* would think that an utterance of *y* by *S* in the circumstances is better evidence that *S* meant that *p*, then *S* will, *ceteris paribus*, utter *x*. And this is just to say that if *S* wants to communicate to *A* that *p* and if *S* thinks that uttering *x* is the surest means available of communicating to *A* that *p*, then, *ceteris paribus*, *S* will utter *x*.

3. It follows from our account of *S*-meaning that an utterance of *x* by *S* will be evidence that *S* meant that *p* by uttering *x* only if

it is mutually known* (or believed*) by S and A that x has a certain feature(s) f as a result of which (or partly as a result of which) x is conspicuously related in a certain way to the belief that p. Obviously, some features are better than others. For example, suppose that S wishes to communicate to A that dinner is ready. Suppose, too, that it is mutual knowledge* between S and A that x has the feature of resembling the type of meat S and A frequently have for dinner and that y has the feature of being an utterance of the same type as that uttered by the cook whenever he means that dinner is ready. While S may be able to communicate to A that dinner is ready either by producing x or by uttering y, it seems clear (at least in the absence of further detail) that uttering y would be for S the surer means of communicating to A that dinner is ready. We might, somewhat metaphorically, mark this difference by saying that the latter feature relates y more *specifically* to the act (type) of meaning that dinner is ready than the former feature relates x to the act (type) of meaning that dinner is ready. The important point to be made here is that, *ceteris paribus*, the more "specifically" a feature f relates x to the act (type) of meaning that p, then—assuming it to be mutually known* by S and A that x is f—the surer x will be as a means for communicating to A that p, and, *a fortiori*, the better will an utterance of x by S be evidence that S meant thereby that p.

Now for a short sketch of how 'grrr' might come to (nc) mean "I am angry" in a rather small group G, one consisting of only two people, S and A, who are stranded together on a desert island without any language or other conventional means of communication.

At time t_1 S desires to communicate to A that he, S, is angry. There is in G no conventional means of communicating that one is angry, but S is rather ingenious. He knows that it is mutual knowledge* between him and A that 'grrr' resembles the sound dogs make when they are angry, and on the strength of this, together with certain facts about the circumstances, S utters 'grrr' with the hope that A will think that S's intention in uttering 'grrr' was to imitate the sound dogs make when they are angry and to understand further that S's intention in doing that was (roughly) to inform A, by means of recognition of intention, that he, S, was angry. We may suppose that S was successful (and that he and A mutually knew* that he was successful) in communicating that he was angry by uttering 'grrr', but that success did not come easily: even when it was clear that he was trying to "tell" A something it took a while before it was realized that S meant that he was angry and not that they were about to be set upon by rabid dogs.

We, as neutral observers, could not have predicted at t_1 what S would utter in order to communicate to A that he was angry. On the other hand, if we know that at some not-too-distant later time, t_2, S again wants to communicate to A that he is angry, we would, I think, predict with a fair degree of confidence that S will utter 'grrr'. In a related manner, we may suppose that at t_1 S was not very confident that 'grrr' would be an efficacious means of communicating to A that S was angry. At t_2, however, we may suppose that S regards 'grrr' as a much surer means of communicating to A that he is angry than it was at t_1; i.e., that at t_2 S will think it is much more likely than it was at t_1 that A will think, on the basis of thinking that S uttered 'grrr', that S meant that he was angry by uttering 'grrr'. Hence, if at t_2 S again wishes to communicate to A that he is angry, he is almost certain, *ceteris paribus*, to do so by uttering 'grrr'.

The increased efficaciousness of 'grrr' as a means of communicating that one is angry is explainable, for the most part, on the basis of (1)–(3) above.

(a) A's position before and after t_1 is not unlike the position of one who sees someone running about in circles, howling at the sky, and who subsequently learns that the person was praying for rain. *Ex hypothesi*, A managed, with difficulty, to guess that S uttered 'grrr' intending thereby to communicate to A that S was angry. The difficulty A had in figuring out what S was up to was due to A's not having prior knowledge of what S believed he could accomplish by uttering 'grrr'. But once this is learned, A will not hesitate (at least not as much as he did at t_1) to make the correct inference the next time S utters 'grrr'; i.e., at t_2, A will, *ceteris paribus*, regard an utterance of 'grrr' by S as being considerably better evidence than he thought it was at t_1 that S meant by uttering 'grrr' that he was angry.

Since it is mutual knowledge* between S and A that at t_1 S meant that he was angry by uttering 'grrr', it is quite likely that S will realize that A now believes that an utterance of 'grrr' by S would now be much better evidence that S meant thereby that he was angry than A believed it to be at t_1. And realizing this S

will regard uttering 'grrr' as a proportionately surer means of communicating to A that he is angry than it was at t_1. Consequently, the probability of S uttering 'grrr' at t_2, given that he wants to communicate to A that he is angry, is proportionately greater than it was at t_1.

Now suppose that A realizes that S realizes that A thinks that the probability of S meaning that he is angry on the assumption that he utters 'grrr' is considerably greater than he thought it was at t_1. A will then realize that S now thinks that 'grrr' is a considerably surer means of communicating to A that S is angry than it was at t_1 and that, consequently, a result of S's realization about A is that S is now even more likely to utter 'grrr' in order to mean that he is angry. But if A thinks that there is a greater probability that S will utter 'grrr' (in certain sorts of circumstances) in order to mean that he is angry, then A will also think that it is now even more probable that if S utters 'grrr' (in certain sorts of circumstances), he will mean thereby that he is angry; i.e., the more likely S is to utter 'grrr' if he wants to communicate to A that he is angry, the better an utterance of 'grrr' by S (in suitable circumstances) is evidence that S meant thereby that he was angry. (Roughly speaking, the more certain a person S is that doing X in circumstances of type C will bring about a certain result e, then given that S did X in circumstances C, the more certain it is that S did X in order to bring about e.)

Should S now realize that A realizes that S realizes that A thinks that the probability of S meaning that he is angry on the assumption that he utters 'grrr' is considerably greater than A thought it was at t_1, then S will realize that this will result in A's thinking that an utterance of 'grrr' by S (in certain sorts of circumstances) would now be even better evidence that S meant thereby that he was angry. Hence, S will now consider 'grrr' an even surer means of communicating to A that S is angry, and therefore, S will be even more likely to utter 'grrr' if he wants to communicate to A that he is angry. Should A now realize that S realizes that A realizes that S realizes . . . And so on, until some natural limit is reached. In short, the more likely S thinks it is that A will infer from the fact that S uttered x that S meant thereby that p, the better and surer will S regard x as a means for communicating to A that p and the more likely it will be that S will utter x in order to communicate to A that p. And the more likely A thinks it is that S will utter x to communicate to A that *p*, the more likely will *A* infer from the fact that *S* uttered *x* that *S* meant thereby that *p*.

(b) The most important factor in 'grrr' becoming a surer and hence more efficacious means of communicating that one is angry is this. A consequence of *S*'s utterance of 'grrr' at t_1 is that the utterance-type 'grrr' will now be mutually known* by *S* and *A* to have a *new feature*, one which it did not have prior to t_1, viz., *that of having beeen uttered by S to mean thereby that he was angry*. It is clear that this new feature of 'grrr' is one which relates 'grrr' much more specifically and directly to the act (type) of meaning that one is angry than does the feature of resembling the sound dogs make when they are angry. Consequently, an utterance of 'grrr' by *S* would now be much better evidence (*ceteris paribus*) that *S* meant thereby that he was angry than it was at t_1. Consequently, 'grrr' is now a proportionately surer means of communicating to *A* that *S* is angry than it was at t_1, and so the probability of *S* uttering 'grrr' if he wants to communicate to *A* that he is angry is considerably greater at t_2 than it was at t_1.

A further result of its being mutual knowledge* between *S* and *A* that 'grrr' has this new feature is that if *A* wishes (at some time after t_1) to communicate to *S* that he, *A*, is angry, *A* will almost certainly do so by uttering 'grrr'. For suppose that at t_2 *A* wishes to communicate to *S* that *A* is angry. Ex *hypothesi*, there is in *G* no conventional means of communicating that one is angry, no utterance-type which means "I am angry". *A* must therefore find some utterance-type *x* which is mutually known* by him and *S* to have a certain feature(s) which relates *x* to the act (type) of meaning that one is angry. Since 'grrr' was at least as good as anything else *S* could think of at t_1, it is unlikely that *A* will be able to think of an utterance-type *x* which has a feature which relates *x* as specifically to the act (type) of meaning that one is angry than does the feature, possessed by 'grrr', of being that uttered by *S* to mean thereby that he was angry. Therefore, it is most likely that *A* will mean that he is angry by uttering 'grrr'.

Assume that at t_2 *A* utters 'grrr' and means thereby that he is angry. This will result in its being mutually known* by *S* and *A* that 'grrr' is what each member of *G* has uttered in order to mean that he was angry. As a result of having *this* new feature, 'grrr' will now be an even surer means in *G* of communicating that one is angry, and so it will now be even more likely that if a member of *G* wants to mean that he is angry, he will do so by uttering 'grrr'. Moreover, it will be mutual knowledge* between S and A that 'grrr' is the *surest* means available for communicating that one is angry. This knowledge will further increase the probability that any member of G will utter 'grrr' in order to communicate that he is angry, and knowledge of this will further fortify and increase the expectation that any member of G will utter 'grrr' if he wants to communicate that he is angry, which in turn will further increase the probability of 'grrr' being uttered if one wants to communicate that one is angry, which in turn will further fortify and increase the expectation that 'grrr' will be uttered if one wants to communicate that one is angry, which in turn will further increase the probability of 'grrr' being uttered if one wants to communicate that one is angry: and so on, until some natural limit is reached.

(c) Suppose that at t_3 each member of G has uttered 'grrr' at least once and that in each case the utterer meant thereby that he was angry. A further result of its being mutually known* by S and A that 'grrr' has this feature is that the ability of a member of G to utter 'grrr' and mean thereby that he was angry will now be considerably less bound by circumstances than it was at t_1. What I mean by this may be illustrated by an example. Suppose that at a not very lively party Mr. Smith manages to communicate to his wife that he is bored by wiggling his ears, and that neither Mr. nor Mrs. Smith know of any other occasion on which someone meant something by wiggling his ears. Undoubtedly, Mr. Smith could not have meant that he was bored by wiggling his ears unless there was a considerable background of mutual knowledge* between him and his wife provided by the circumstances, e.g., that the party was not lively, that he was not in a position to say that he was bored, etc. Smith could not at that time have meant that he was bored by wiggling his ears if he had been sitting at home reading a book. However, *after* having meant that he was bored by wiggling his ears at the party, it is quite possible that he could *then* mean that he is bored by wiggling his ears while sitting at home reading a book.

Why this should be so is explainable in the following way. Suppose that in virtue of having a certain feature f an utterance-type x is related in way R to the propositions p_1, p_2, and p_3. If, now, S is to mean that p_1 by uttering x in virtue of x being f, then he must think that A is provided with certain information which will enable him to eliminate p_2 and p_3 as the propositions he is intended to believe. Such information may be that it is mutually known* by S and A that p_2 and p_3 are irrelevant, false or true. But S could only mean that p_1 by uttering x in circumstances which were such as to make the elimination of p_2 and p_3 possible, independently of S uttering x. Suppose, however, that x comes to have a new feature, f', as a result of which x is related in way R' only to p_1 and that R' relates x more specifically to the act of meaning that p_1 than R relates x to the act of meaning that p_1 or the act of meaning that p_2 or the act of meaning that p_3. In this case S will be considerably less bound by circumstances in his ability to mean that p_1 by uttering x.

Thus, at t_1 the only relevant feature for the identification of the proposition S intended to communicate to A by uttering 'grrr' was the feature of resembling the sound dogs make when they are angry. But this feature relates 'grrr' in more or less the same way to several propositions, so S was heavily dependent on the circumstances for disambiguation. The effect of its being mutually known* by S and A that 'grrr' now has the feature of having been uttered by each to mean thereby that the utterer was angry is that either of them is able to communicate to the other that he is angry by uttering 'grrr' in a greater variety of circumstances. This lack of restriction will further increase the likelihood of a member of G uttering 'grrr' if he wants to communicate that he is angry. Moreover, a further result of this "spreading" effect may be that it increases the probability that a member of G will actually mean that he is angry (by uttering 'grrr'); for the will often waits only for the way.

A further consequence of the repeated use of 'grrr' to mean that one is angry, a consequence implicit in what has already been said, is that the more 'grrr' is used to mean that one is angry, the less likely will one be to utter 'grrr' unless he means thereby that he is angry; for each will know that if he utters 'grrr' in the presence of the other, the latter is quite likely, *ceteris paribus*, to think that by uttering 'grrr' the utterer meant that he was angry; so one will, *ceteris paribus*, refrain from uttering 'grrr' unless one wants this inference made. (There will, however, inevitably be circumstances in which one can utter 'grrr' in the presence of another without meaning that one is angry, e.g., when it is perfectly obvious that one is not angry. Quite likely this tells us something about the origin of figurative speech.)

On the assumption that members of G continue, not too infrequently, to have occasion to communicate that they are angry, we should expect that before long it will be mutual knowledge* amongst the members of G that it has been the practice in G to utter 'grrr' when and only when one means that one is angry. This will result, for the reasons given above, in the continued use of 'grrr' when and only when one means that one is angry, which in turn will result in there continuing to be a practice in G of uttering 'grrr' when and only when one means that one is angry, which in turn will result in the continued use of 'grrr' when and only when one means that one is angry . . . And so on, until they either hit upon a more efficient system of communication or become a great deal more complacent. Self-perpetuating regularities of this type are, as we shall see in section V.3, conventions, and at this point we may say that 'grrr' (*nc*) means "I am angry" in G.

While it seems reasonable to suppose that

> x (*nc*) means "p" in G if it is mutual knowledge* amongst the members of G that
>
> (1) it has been the practice in G to mean that p by uttering x and to utter x only when one means thereby that p, and, at least partly in virtue of (1),
>
> (2) members of G will, when they mean that p, mean that p by uttering x and will utter x only when they mean thereby that p,

these conditions are not necessary.

(1) It is not necessary that whenever a member of G means that p, he means that p by uttering x. There may be some other utterance-type which also means "p" in G.

(2) It is not necessary that members of G utter x only when they mean thereby that p. It may be that in addition to (*nc*) meaning "p", x also (*nc*) means "q" in G, or even that x has some other use unconnected with communication.

It may seem that the moral to be drawn from these two points is that an account of what it is for x to (*nc*) mean "p" in G need only require that it be mutual knowledge* amongst the members of G that there is *a* precedent in G of uttering x to mean thereby that p (i.e., that some members of G have meant that p by uttering x) and, on the basis of this precedent, any member of G who intends to communicate that p to any other member of G may do so, *ceteris paribus*, by uttering x. In other words, it may seem that

x will (nc) mean "p" in G just in case x is in G an efficacious means of communicating that p and this because it is mutual knowledge* amongst the members of G that x has the feature of being that by the utterance of which members of G have meant that p.

Unfortunately, this proposed revision provides neither a necessary nor a sufficient condition for x (nc) meaning "p" in G.

To see that a sufficient condition is not provided, suppose that it is mutual knowledge* amongst the members of G that x (nc) means "p" in G', a small subclass of G (say, a certain family or sect), but that no member of G who is not also a member of G' would consider uttering x. In such a case it may be that any member of G *could*—on the basis of its being mutual knowledge* in G that members of G' mean that p by uttering x—mean that p by uttering x. Nevertheless, it would not, I think, be true to say that in such a case x would (nc) mean "p" in G. What precludes x, in this example, from meaning "p" in G, despite there being a precedent in G for uttering x to mean thereby that p, is that there is no expectation at all on the part of members of G that those members of G who are not members of G' will utter x in order to mean that p. If x is to (nc) mean "p" in G there must, it would seem, be at least some likelihood that any member of G who wants to communicate that p to any other member of G will do so by uttering x; were there no tendency or propensity at all on the part of most members of G to utter x when they mean that p, then x would not (nc) means "p" in G. So perhaps we may say that x (nc) means "p" in G if it is mutual knowledge* amongst the members of G that (1) there is a precedent in G for uttering x to mean thereby that p, and, on the basis (in part) of (1), (2) any member of G who means that p *might* do so by uttering x.

But it is not necessary that there be any precedent in G for uttering x; for it may be that x (nc) means "p" in G even though no member of G ever meant anything by uttering x. For example, the members of G may have agreed to whistle in a certain way if ever they are attacked, but, having friendly neighbours, the occasion has never arisen. (Air-raid sirens in North America, so far, provide an actual example.) What is shown here is that while almost always if x (nc) means "p" in G, x will be an efficacious means of communicating that p by virtue of there being a precedent for uttering x to mean thereby that p, still, an agreement (or explicit and mutual avowals) to mean that p by uttering x, or to utter x only when one means thereby that p, or an agreement (or stipulation) that if one utters x one may mean thereby that p, will also suffice to secure that x (nc) means "p" in G. (Of course, a convention which begins by agreement will, once the original agreement is forgotten, come to be sustained by precedent.)

I believe that what precedent and agreement (or stipulation) have in common such that they and they alone may serve as the relevant feature f of x, if x is to (nc) mean "p" in G is, quite roughly, that both entail an overt or public *acceptance* of x as a means of communicating that p. While members of G may be *able* to mean that p by uttering x in virtue of some "natural" feature possessed by x, they have not thereby adopted or accepted x as a suitable means of communicating that p. And if this is only part of the story, the other part—which probably entails the first part—is surely that these are the best possible features an utterance-type can have if it is to serve as a means of communicating that p.

Finally, we are in a position to say what it is for x to (nc) mean "p" in G. The following notational convenience, borrowed from Grice's "Utterer's Meaning, Sentence-Meaning, and Word-Meaning", will render the statement of our definition simpler: let 'S uttered x M-intending to produce in A the activated belief that p' be equivalent to the analysans of my account of what it is for S to mean that p by uttering x. We may now say that

x (nc) means "p" in G iff it is mutual knowledge* amongst the members of G that

(1) if almost any member of G utters something M-intending to produce in some other member of G the activated belief that p, then what he utters might be x;

(2) if any member of G utters x M-intending to produce in some other member of G the activated belief that p, he will intend the state of affairs E (which he intends to realize by uttering x) to include the fact that x is such that there is a precedent in G for uttering x and meaning thereby that p (or an agreement (or stipulation) in G that x may be uttered to mean thereby that p).

Comments

1. The qualification "almost any" as it appears in the definition is to allow for some members of G who do not share the interests

common to the other members of G, or who simply refuse, for one reason or another, to utter x. A similar restriction might seem to be in order for the requirement that conditions (1) and (2) be mutual knowledge* amongst *all* members of G: we do not want to require such knowledge of infants and morons. But here I propose to borrow from a suggestion put forward by David K. Lewis,[1] and to treat the mutual knowledge* condition as partially defining membership in group G (thus G might consist of all normal adult people who live in a certain area).

2. How is one to understand the phrase 'mutual knowledge* amongst the members of G'? Does this mean that each member of G knows of each member of G that he knows . . .? Or does it merely mean that every member of G knows that anyone who is a member of G knows that . . .? The mutual knowledge* condition must be taken in the second of these two senses. That is, to say that conditions (1) and (2) are mutual knowledge* amongst the members of G is to say:

$$(x) (Gx \rightarrow Kx(1)-(2)) \ \&$$
$$Kx(y) (Gy \rightarrow Ky(1)-(2))) \ \&$$
$$Kx(y) (Gy \rightarrow Ky(z) (Gz \rightarrow Kz(1)-(2)))) \ \& . \quad . \quad .$$

It follows from conditions (1) and (2) that members of G are able to recognize one another as members of G; but it would be absurd to require that every member of G have knowledge of each member of G.

3. A consequence of our definition is that x (nc) means "p" in G if and only if it is mutual knowledge* amongst the members of G that x (nc) means "p" in G; for, necessarily, if it is mutual knowledge* amongst the members of G that p, then it is mutual knowledge* amongst the members of G that it is mutual knowledge* amongst the members of G that p. This partly explains the fact—which some find problematic for an account of meaning which takes S-meaning as primary—that one knows what S meant by uttering x on the basis of knowing what x means.

4. An account of what it is for x to (nc) mean "so-and-so is to ψ" in G may be given which is *mutatis mutandis* identical with our account of what it is for x to (nc) mean "p" in G. And I submit—with some arguments forthcoming in section VI.1— that it is misleading but correct, subject to a certain qualification,

---

[1] *Convention*, pp. 76–7.

to say that x (nc) means something in G just in case x (nc) means "p" in G or x (nc) means "so-and-so is to ψ" in G.

Not surprisingly, my account of non-composite whole-utterance types is similar in some important respects to an account of non-composite whole-utterance types offered by Grice in his recent article, "Utterer's Meaning, Sentence-Meaning, and Word-Meaning".[2] But the two accounts are also dissimilar in some important respects, and for at least this reason it will be helpful briefly to consider Grice's account. But before going into Grice's account, a comment and a simplification are in order.

(1) Grice's account of utterance-meaning is given in terms of a revised version of his 1957 account of S-meaning. The important revision for our purpose is that whereas Grice in 1957 wanted to say that S meant that p by uttering x just in case S uttered x intending to produce in A the belief that p by means of recognition of intention, the intended response in 1968 is A's thinking that S thinks that p. Grice uses the phrase '[S] uttered x M-intending A to think that [S] thinks that p' as an abbreviation for the original three-pronged definiens (as revised).

(2) Grice's definienda are of the form 'X means "$*\psi p$"', where the device '$*\psi$' (read 'asterisk-sub-Ψ') is a dummy

> which represents a specific mood-indicator which corresponds to the propositional attitude Ψ-ing (whichever that may be), as for example, '⊢' corresponds to believing (thinking) and '!' corresponds to intending. (Op. cit., p. 230.)

For our purposes this will not be needed, and I will use my own terminology and give Grice's definition only as it applies to 'x (nc) means "p" in G'.

Grice does not begin with an account of what it is for x to (nc) mean "p" in G. He first offers an account of what it is for x to (nc) mean "p" *for a particular individual S* (within S's idiolect), and it is primarily on the basis of this account that Grice offers his account of what it is for x to (nc) mean "p" in a group G.

As a first shot, Grice suggests that 'x (nc) means "p" for S' may be defined as 'It is S's policy (practice, habit) to utter x if S is making an utterance by which S *means that p*'; i.e., 'It is S's policy (practice, habit) to utter x if S is making an utterance by means of which (for some A) S M-intends to effect that A thinks

---

[2] Grice uses the word 'unstructured' where I use 'non-composite'.

S to think that *p*'. But Grice argues that even if this definiens is otherwise acceptable, "the notion of *M*-intention is otiose here, and . . . only the notion of simple intention [i.e., the simple intention to produce in *A* the belief that *S* thinks that *p*] need be invoked" (ibid., p. 232). For if it is *S*'s policy to utter *x* if *S* intends some audience to think *S* thinks that *p*, then "it will follow that when, on a given occasion, he utters [*x*], he will do so, on that occasion, *M*-intending to affect his audience in that way" (ibid.). The reason Grice thinks that this follows is that if *S* is to have the particular intentions involved in every implementation of his policy, then he must be in a position, when uttering *x*, to suppose that there is some chance that his intentions will be realized. But for such a supposition to be justified, Grice argues, "a given audience *A* must be aware of [*S*'s] policy and must suppose it to apply to the utterance of [*x*] with which [*S*] has presented him" (ibid.). Therefore, if it is *S*'s policy to utter *x* if he intends some *A* to think that *S* thinks that *p*, then, whenever *S* utters *x*, he will utter *x* expecting *A* to infer from the fact that it is *S*'s policy to utter *x* intending to produce in some *A* the belief that *S* thinks that *p* that *S* has this particular intention on this particular occasion and to infer therefrom that *S* thinks that *p*. Thus, a formulation of *S*'s policy in terms of simple intention secures that by a particular utterance of *x*, *S* will mean that *p*.

By this route, Grice arrives at the following simplified definition.

> For *S*, *x* (*nc*) means "*p*" iff it is *S*'s policy (practice, habit) to utter *x* if, for some *A*, *S* intends (wants) *A* to think that *S* thinks that *p*.

But this definition is found to be unacceptable for two reasons. (1) For *S*, *x* may have some meaning other than "*p*"; so it cannot be *S*'s policy to utter *x* *only if* he wants some *A* to think *S* thinks that *p*. (2) *S* may have some other utterance-type by which he also means that *p*; so it cannot be *S*'s policy to utter *x* *if* he wants some *A* to think *S* thinks that *p*. To cope with these difficulties, Grice employs the notion of "having a certain procedure in one's repertoire". Grice's explanation of this notion is given by example.

A faintly eccentric lecturer might have in his repertoire the following procedure: if he sees an attractive girl in his audience, to pause for half a minute and then take a sedative. His having in his repertoire this procedure would not be incompatible with his also having two further procedures: (a) if he sees an attractive girl, to put on a pair of dark spectacles (instead of pausing and taking a sedative); (b) to pause and take a sedative when he sees in his audience not an attractive girl, but a particularly distinguished colleague. (Ibid., p. 233.)

Similarly, *S*'s having in his repertoire the procedure of uttering *x* if he wants some *A* to think *S* thinks that *p* is not incompatible with his having in his repertoire two further procedures: (a) to utter *y* if he wants some *A* to think *S* thinks that *p*; and (b) to utter *x* if he wants some *A* to think *S* thinks that *q*.

So Grice suggests that:

> For *S*, *x* (*nc*) means "*p*" iff *S* has in his repertoire the following procedure: to utter a token of *x* if, for some *A*, *S* intends (wants) *A* to think that *S* thinks that *p*. (Ibid.)

Where *x* (*nc*) means "*p*" for a group of individuals, Grice suggests:

> *x* (*nc*) means "*p*" in group *G* iff at least some (? many) members of group *G* have in their repertoires the procedure of uttering a token of *x* if, for some *A*, they want *A* to think they think that *p*; the retention of this procedure being for them conditional on the assumption that at least some (other) members of *G* have, or have had, this procedure in their repertoires. (Ibid.)

Neither of these definitions provides sufficient conditions. Consider Grice's account of what it is for *x* to (*nc*) mean "*p*" for a particular individual *S*. It is possible for *S* to satisfy the analysans without ever meaning anything by uttering *x*. For example, *S* might have a special drug which he surreptitiously puts in someone's tea whenever he wants that person to think that *S* thinks that that person is wonderful; or *S*'s policy might be to salivate whenever he wants someone to think that *S* (thinks *S*) is hungry. The problem, of course, is that Grice is wrong in claiming that it will *follow* from *S*'s having the policy of uttering *x* if he intends *A* to think that *S* thinks that *p* that whenever *S* utters *x* he will intend to produce in *A* this belief by means of *A*'s recognition of *S*'s intention. There are more ways to produce in someone a belief than by means of recognition of intention.

The same objection applies to Grice's account of what it is for *x* to (*nc*) mean "*p*" in *G*. Thus, it might be the policy of every member of *G* to simulate a belch (i.e., to pretend he is really belching) if he wants some *A* to think that he (thinks he) enjoyed his meal; but each member of G has this policy because he thinks everyone else does, although each member of G thinks he is the only person who is aware that everyone has this policy.

Nor will sufficiency be secured by merely reverting to Grice's first suggestion and replacing the "simple" intention with the relevant M-intentions. For, to take first the case of x (nc) meaning "p" in S's idiolect, it might be S's policy to utter 'grrr' if S M-intends to produce in some A the belief that S (thinks S) is angry, but that S relies not on A's knowledge of S's policy, but on A's ability, on each occasion that S utters 'grrr', to infer S's intentions on the basis of 'grrr' resembling the sound dogs make. Similarly for the case of x (nc) meaning "p" in group G: it is, we imagine, the policy of each member of G to utter 'grrr' if he M-intends some other member of G to think he (thinks he) is angry; each member of G has this policy because he thinks that every other member of G has this policy, but each member of G mistakenly thinks that he alone knows that every other member of G has this policy. Consequently, whenever any member of G utters 'grrr' he intends his audience to infer his intentions on the basis of the audience's belief that 'grrr' resembles the sound dogs make when they are angry.

Now in the examples in the preceding paragraph, 'grrr' fails to mean "I am angry", either for S or for G, because it is only on the basis of 'grrr' having a "natural" feature that people are able to mean by uttering 'grrr' that they are angry. So (taking now only the case of x (nc) meaning "p" in G) it may seem that Grice's definition may be adequately repaired by explicitly requiring that members of G intend the relevant inference to be made from the fact that one uttered x on the basis of A's knowledge of one's procedure of uttering x if one M-intends A to think that one thinks that p. But even this will not suffice, for at the next level of complication we have the following situation. Each member of G has the policy of uttering 'grrr' if he M-intends some A to think he (thinks he) is angry; each member of G has this policy because he thinks every other member of G has this policy; and each member of G thinks that every member of G thinks that every member of G has this policy. But each member of G mistakenly thinks that each other member of G mistakenly thinks that he alone knows that every other member of G has this policy. Consequently, whenever a member of G, S, utters 'grrr', he intends some A to think that S intends A to think that S (thinks S) is angry on the

K

basis of A's knowledge of S's policy, but he also intends A mistakenly to think that S intends A's inference to be made on the basis of A's thinking that 'grrr' resembles the sound dogs make when they are angry. That is, S intends A to reason: "S uttered 'grrr'. It is S's policy to utter 'grrr' if S M-intends someone to think S (thinks S) is angry. But S is unaware that I know of his policy; so his intention in uttering 'grrr' is that I should infer therefrom his intention that I should think he (thinks he) is angry on the basis, in part, of 'grrr' resembling the sound dogs make when they are angry."

Now the moral of all this is, I think, that Grice will have a sufficient condition for x (nc) meaning "p" in G only if it is specified that it is mutual knowledge* amongst the members of G that most members of G have in their repertoire the procedure of uttering x if, for some A, they M-intend A to think they think that p. It may then seem to be a consequence of such a revision that an utterance of x will make known S's M-intention to produce in A the belief that S thinks that p on the basis of its being mutual knowledge* amongst the members of G that members of G have this procedure in their repertoire. But what more can it mean to say that members of G have this procedure in their repertoire than that members of G might utter x if, for some A, they M-intend A to think they think that p? But if this is so, then it will be mutual knowledge* in G that members of G have this procedure at least partly on the basis of its being mutual knowledge* that at least some members of G have uttered x and meant thereby that p. And should we revise Grice's account along these lines, his clause specifying that each member's retention of the procedure is contingent on other members of G having this procedure will be superfluous and a consequence of the definition so revised.

V.2 *Co-ordination problems*

In the preceding section I claimed that if x meets the conditions I offered for (nc) meaning "p" in a group G, then x will be in G a conventional means of communicating that p. At one point I suggested that frequently if x (nc) means "p" in G, then there will be a convention in G to mean that p by uttering x, or a convention to utter x only when one means thereby that p. Thus, whether x (nc) means "p" in G is a matter of convention, the conventions which prevail in G with respect to x—not, I admit, a very original thesis.

I propose now to offer a general account of convention, one arrived at, as it were, by extraction from the account given of what it is for *x* to (*nc*) mean something in a group *G* (although the account of convention will apply as well to composite whole-utterance types, though not, of course, in exactly the same way). Since arriving at this account of convention, I have had the pleasure of reading David Lewis's book, *Convention*. Lewis's account of convention is, he notes, similar in important respects to an account put forward some time ago by David Hume, who said that a convention is:

. . . a general sense of common interest; which sense all the members of the society express to one another, and which induces them to regulate their conduct by certain rules. I observe, that [e.g.] it will be for my interest to leave another in the possession of his goods, *provided* he will act in the same manner with regard to me. He is sensible of a like interest in the regulation of his conduct. When this common sense of interest is mutually expressed, and is known to both, it produces a suitable resolution and behaviour. And this may properly enough be called a convention or agreement betwixt us, though without the interposition of a promise; since the actions of each of us have a reference to those of the other, and are performed upon the supposition that something is to be performed on the other part.[3]

Since I believe that Hume's account is not too far from being essentially correct, I have something in common with Lewis. What I should like to borrow from Lewis is his idea of arriving at an account of convention via the theory of games.

Lewis's analysis of convention has its source in the theory of games of pure co-ordination, as developed by T. C. Schelling in his book, *The Strategy of Conflict*. The theory of games of pure co-ordination is a part of the general theory of games of von Neumann and Morgenstern. Games theory is concerned with games of strategy, as opposed to games of skill or games of chance. Games of strategy are situations involving two or more people in which each agent's best course of action is dependent upon what he expects the others involved with him in that situation to do, each of them knowing, in turn, that each agent's best course of action is determined by what he expects the others to do. The term 'strategy' is "intended to focus on the interdependence of the [agents'] decisions and on their expectations about each other's

---

[3] *A Treatise of Human Nature*, III. ii. 2.

behavior".[4] It is convenient to think of the games of strategy as lying somewhere between two poles. At one end we have *games of pure conflict* ("zero-sum games"), where the agents' preferences are perfectly correlated inversely, and at the other end we have *games of pure co-ordination*, where the agents' preferences are perfectly correlated positively. In between lies *the mixed-motive game*, e.g., standard bargaining problems. (The mixed-motive and pure-co-ordination games make up the "non-zero-sum games".) In both games of pure conflict and games of pure co-ordination each agent does what he does on the basis of what he expects the others to do. The difference is that in a game of pure conflict, e.g., one person hunting another person, each agent tries to do that which he expects the others *not* to expect him to do, whereas in a game of pure co-ordination, e.g., two people seeking to meet, each agent tries to do that which he expects the others to expect him to do.

It should be remarked at the outset that while I think Lewis's idea of approaching an account of convention via the theory of games of pure co-ordination very helpful, in itself and for my own ends, I do not think (as will be clear in section V.3) that a complete account of convention can be given in terms of the theory of games of pure co-ordination, and the account I shall arrive at differs significantly from that arrived at by Lewis.

Let us begin with some examples of the type of situation which Schelling and Lewis call "co-ordination problems".[5] Eventually we shall see that one type of convention is a regularity in the behaviour of members of a group *G* which constitutes a solution to a recurrent co-ordination problem.

1. Two people are each told to write some positive number without communicating with one another. If they both write the same number, they will each receive $10, otherwise they receive nothing.

Neither agent will care which number he writes, just so long as it is the same number the other writes. Thus, each must try to guess what the other will do, and decide what he will do on the basis of what he thinks the other will do. But John does not simply try to guess what Tom will write, since Tom will write

---

[4] Schelling, *The Strategy of Conflict*, p. 3.

[5] Examples (1)–(3) are from Schelling, *The Strategy of Conflict*; (3) and a version of (4) are also in Lewis, *Convention*.

what he guesses John will write. So the question each has to ask is not simply, "What would I write if I were he?", but, "What would I write if I were he wondering what he would write if he were I wondering what I would write if I were he . . . ?"[6]

2. Two parachutists land unexpectedly in the area shown in the map below. It is mutual knowledge* between them that they are in this area and that each has the same map of the area. But neither knows where within this area the other is, nor are they able to communicate. They must rendezvous as soon as possible to be rescued.

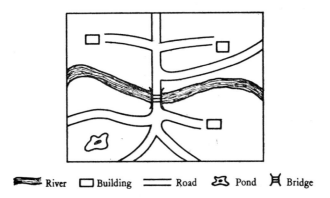

⬛ River   ☐ Building   ══ Road   ☒ Pond   Ħ Bridge

3. Two people are suddenly cut off in the middle of their telephone conversation. It is mutually believed* by them that each wants the connection restored so that the conversation may be continued.

In the preceding two examples, each agent had to do the "same act" ("same" under some specially relevant description) if co-ordination was to be achieved. In this case, the agents will achieve co-ordination only if one decides to wait while the other decides to call; for if both call back they get an "engaged" signal, and if both wait for the other to call they cannot resume their conversation. We may presume that neither cares whether he calls or waits, just so long as he succeeds in co-ordinating his action with that of the other, thereby achieving a restoration of their telephone connection.

In examples (1)–(3) communication between the agents in adopting a course of action is precluded. In examples (4) and (5) communication, and therefore agreement, is possible.

[6] Schelling, *The Strategy of Conflict*, p. 54.

4. A group of people of mixed nationality (some English, some American) set up a community in some unsettled place. Since they brought their cars, they want to secure that they drive without fear of collision. No one cares whether he drives on the right or the left side of the road, so long as the side he drives on is the same side everyone else drives on.

5. The people in a new housing development want their rubbish collected. The city does not want it lying around, so wants to collect it. Thus there is a mutual or shared interest in the collection of rubbish. The people do not care which day they put out their rubbish, so long as it is the same day it is collected. The city does not care which day they come by to collect the rubbish, so long as it is the same day it is put out.

In each of the examples (1)–(5), each agent involved in the co-ordination problem desires to bring about a certain good or desires to avoid a certain evil. To achieve the desired end each agent must choose one of several alternative and mutually incompatible courses of action. He cares little which course of action he adopts, just that it be that course of action which when combined with the actions of the other agents involved will bring about their desired end; for the end desired by each of the agents is jointly determined by their managing to co-ordinate their behaviour in one or another of several alternative and mutually incompatible ways. In the terms of the theory of games, in each of the above problems some combinations of agents' actions are *equilibria*: combinations of agents' actions such that the action of each agent is the best strategy (or as good as any other) that can be coupled with the actions of the other agents involved; combinations of agents' actions which are such that, given the actions of the others, each agent has done as well as he could. In an equilibrium combination no one agent could have done better, unless the other agents had acted otherwise.[7] (Suppose that in problem (2) the parachutists succeed in meeting at the bridge. It may be that one of them would have preferred meeting at the pond, since that was closer to where he landed; but, given that the other parachutist went to the bridge, he prefers going to the bridge to any other course of action.)

The concept of an equilibrium may be illustrated by drawing *payoff matrices* for co-ordination problems between two people.

---

[7] Lewis, *Convention*, p. 8; Schelling, *The Strategy of Conflict*, p. 292.

Call the agents *Row-chooser* and *Column-chooser*. We represent Row-chooser's alternative actions by labeled rows of the matrix, and Column-chooser's by labeled columns. The squares then represent combinations of the agents' actions and the expected outcomes thereof. Squares are labeled with two *payoffs*, numbers somehow measuring the desirability of the expected outcome for Row-chooser and Column-chooser. Row-chooser's payoff is at the lower left, Column-chooser's is at the upper right.[8]

Matrix #1 represents a simplified version of problem (2), and matrix #2 represents problem (3).

	C_1	C_2	C_3
R_1	1 / 1	0 / 0	0 / 0
R_2	0 / 0	1 / 1	0 / 0
R_3	0 / 0	0 / 0	1 / 1

#1

	C_1	C_2
R_1	1 / 1	0 / 0
R_2	0 / 0	1 / 1

#2

In matrix #1, R_1, R_2, and R_3 are Row-chooser's alternative actions of going to places P_1, P_2, and P_3 respectively. C_1, C_2, and C_3 represent Column-chooser's actions of going to places P_1, P_2, and P_3 respectively. Thus, $\langle R_1, C_1 \rangle$ represents Row-chooser's and Column-chooser's combined actions of going to place P_1, and $\langle R_2, C_1 \rangle$ represents that combination of actions in which Row-chooser goes to place P_2 and Column-chooser goes to place P_1. The equilibria are the three combinations $\langle R_1, C_1 \rangle$, $\langle R_2, C_2 \rangle$, and $\langle R_3, C_3 \rangle$, the three combinations in which Row-chooser and Column-chooser go to the same place and meet. In matrix #2, R_1 and R_2 represent Row-chooser's alternative actions of calling back and waiting respectively; and C_1 and C_2 represent Column-chooser's alternative actions of waiting and calling back respectively. Thus, the equilibria are $\langle R_1, C_1 \rangle$ and $\langle R_2, C_2 \rangle$: the former is that combination in which Row-chooser calls back and Column-chooser waits, thereby restoring the connection, and the latter is that combination in which Row-chooser waits and Column-chooser calls back, thereby restoring the connection.

[8] Lewis, *Convention*, p. 9.

$\langle R2, C1 \rangle$ is that combination in which each agent waits for the other to call back.

Not all equilibria are co-ordination equilibria, as is shown by the pure conflict game represented in matrix #3.

	$C1$	$C2$
$R1$	0 / 0	−2 / 2
$R2$	2 / −2	−1 / 1

#3

Here, $\langle R1, C1 \rangle$ is an equilibrium, for each agent's strategy is as good as any other that can be coupled with the other's: given that Column-chooser adopts $C1$, Row-chooser has no better strategy than to adopt $R1$, and given that Row-chooser adopts $R1$, Column-chooser has no better strategy than to adopt $C1$.

An equilibrium is a combination in which no one would have been better off had he alone acted otherwise. Lewis defines a *co-ordination equilibrium*

as a combination in which no one would have been better off had *any one* agent alone acted otherwise, either himself or someone else. Co-ordination equilibria are equilibria, by the definitions. Equilibria in games of pure coordination are always coordination equilibria, since the agents' interests coincide perfectly. (Ibid., p. 14.)

Thus, $\langle R1, C1 \rangle$ in matrix #3 is an equilibrium but not a co-ordination equilibrium: Row-chooser would have been better off had Column-chooser adopted $C2$, and Column-chooser would have been better off had Row-chooser adopted $R2$. But co-ordination equilibria can occur in games of pure conflict: $\langle R1, C1 \rangle$ in matrix #4 is a co-ordination equilibrium.[9]

	$C1$	$C2$
$R1$	0 / 0	0 / 0
$R2$	0 / 0	−1 / 1

#4

[9] Lewis, *Convention*, p. 15.

Even if we ignore the "degenerate" case in which a co-ordination equilibrium occurs in a game of pure conflict, the fact that a situation possesses a co-ordination equilibrium would still not provide a sufficient condition for that situation constituting a co-ordination *problem*. (At least this is what Lewis wants to say, and I will go along with him.) There are at least two types of cases it seems desirable to exclude. (1) Situations occur in which there is only one co-ordination equilibrium. In such cases co-ordination is not a *problem*. (2) There are, however, cases possessing two co-ordination equilibria which are equally as trivial as those having only one—for example, the game represented in matrix #5.

#5

Here, ⟨R1, C1⟩ and ⟨R1, C2⟩ are co-ordination equilibria, but there is no more difficulty in achieving co-ordination in this case than in a case involving only one co-ordination equilibrium. In matrix #5 the equilibria ⟨R1, C1⟩ and ⟨R1, C2⟩ are equivalent and interchangeable.

Equilibrium pairs are *equivalent* if, for each player separately, they yield equal payoffs; equilibrium pairs are *interchangeable* if all pairs formed from the corresponding strategies are also equilibrium points [i.e., equilibria]. (They are therefore equivalent and interchangeable only if all pairs formed from the corresponding strategies are equivalent.)[10]

However, there is nothing wrong with a co-ordination problem having two or more equivalent and interchangeable co-ordination equilibria, provided that *not all* of its co-ordination equilibria are equivalent and interchangeable.

We might now say that, roughly:

Two or more people are agents in a co-ordination problem iff it is mutual knowledge* (belief*) amongst them that

[10] Schelling, *The Strategy of Conflict*, p. 292.

(1) there is a certain (usually "shared") end which each
    desires to achieve, and
(2) each will achieve his end if and only if each co-ordinates
    his action with the actions of the other agents involved in
    one of two or more alternative and mutually incompatible
    ways, i.e., at least two combinations of agents' actions
    are co-ordination equilibria which are not both equiva-
    lent and interchangeable.

The need for the "mutual knowledge*" condition results from
the desirability of distinguishing, e.g., the "parachutist" example
from such degenerate versions as might arise if both agents
desire to meet, but A thinks that B is without a map, or A thinks
that B thinks that A is without a map, or A thinks that B thinks
that A thinks that B is without a map, etc., thereby rendering
co-ordination impossible, unless they achieve it by chance.

There are certain consequences of this analysis of co-ordination
problems worth noticing. Once this is done we will be in a position to show how one type of convention might come about.
(It will be assumed throughout that it is always mutual knowledge*
amongst the agents involved in a co-ordination problem that
each is as rational as any normal person.)
(1) The first consequence of note is that each agent in a co-
ordination problem will adopt that course of action which he
thinks the others expect him to adopt (if there is a particular
action he thinks they *expect* him to adopt); each will do what he
thinks the others expect him to expect them to expect him to do;
each will do what he thinks the others expect him to expect them
to expect him to expect them to expect him to do; and so on.
This may be illustrated by an example.
Two people, Ralph and Cynthia, are agents in a co-ordination
problem of the sort represented in matrix #1. Since they are
agents in that co-ordination problem, it is mutual knowledge*
between them that each wants to meet with the other and that
they will succeed in meeting if and only if both go at the same
time to either P_1 or P_2 or P_3 and that both are indifferent as to
where they go, so long as they meet. Suppose now that Ralph
expects Cynthia to go to P_1. He will therefore go to P_1. Suppose
that Ralph thinks that Cynthia expects him to go to P_1. He will
therefore expect her to go to P_1, and therefore he will go to

P_1. Suppose that Ralph thinks that Cynthia expects him to expect her to go to P_1. He believes that since she expects him to expect her to go to P_1, she will therefore expect him to go to P_1, and since she expects him to go to P_1, she will go to P_1. Therefore, he will go to P_1. Suppose that Ralph thinks that Cynthia expects him to expect her to expect him to go to P_1. He believes that since she expects him to expect her to expect him to go to P_1, she will expect him to expect her to go to P_1, and therefore she will expect him to go to P_1, and therefore she will go to P_1. Therefore he will go to P_1. And so on.

(2) Agents in a co-ordination problem may not be able to form rational expectations about which course of action the others will adopt, but in that case they will not have much more than a random chance of achieving co-ordination. It is clearly in their best interests to try to calculate what the others will do. If it is mutual knowledge* (belief*) amongst them what each expects the others to do, then co-ordination is virtually assured. In those cases where communication is not precluded (e.g., problems (4) and (5) above), achieving co-ordination will not be at all problematic: the agents involved will form the necessary expectations on the basis of an explicit agreement to conform to a particular co-ordination equilibrium. But agents in a co-ordination problem manage to form the necessary expectations, and so achieve co-ordination, even when they are unable to communicate with one another. Thus, agents in problem (1) are not unlikely to suspect that each will write the number one; agents involved in problem (2) will almost certainly expect one another to go to the bridge; and agents involved in problem (3) are likely to expect one another to expect the original caller to call back.

On what basis do agents form their expectations in such cases? Clearly, they do so on the basis of one co-ordination equilibrium being conspicuously different from the others in some especially relevant way; frequently the common situation provides "some clue for coordinating behaviour, some focal point for each person's expectation of what the other expects him to expect to be expected to do" (ibid., p. 57). Thus, in problem (1) it may be mutually obvious that the universe of all positive numbers has a "beginning" or "first" or "smallest" number but no "middle" or "end". In the parachutists' problem it will no doubt be mutually recognized that while there are several buildings and intersections, there is only one bridge (there is only one pond, but it is not so centrally located and there is no road leading to it). In the "telephone" problem it may occur to each agent (and occur to each that it will occur to each, etc.) that at least the original caller knows the other's number or knows how to find it.

Agents in a co-ordination problem, we may say, mutually expect* one another to seek a co-ordination equilibrium that possesses a certain feature(s) which makes that co-ordination equilibrium the rational choice. What conditions must such a feature meet if it is to provide the agents with a basis for forming expectations about what each expects the others to do? This question may be put in another way. Suppose that a certain co-ordination equilibrium X has a certain feature f. What must be the case if the fact that X is f is to serve as a basis for each agent's expecting the other agents involved to adopt co-ordination equilibrium X? (i) It must be mutually known* or believed* by the agents involved that X is f. The fact that there is only one bridge (in problem (2)) will be useless to A unless he thinks that B is aware that there is only one bridge; by the same token, A knows that this fact is useless to B unless B thinks that A thinks that there is only one bridge; and so on, *ad infinitum*. (ii) It is not enough that the agents involved in a co-ordination problem mutually know* that X is f; for it may not *occur* to them that X is f (e.g., agents involved in problem (1) will no doubt know that the number one is the first member of the series of all positive numbers, but unless this knowledge is activated it will be useless for their solution to the problem). So a second condition is that the agents mutually know* (or believe*) that it is conspicuous to all the agents involved that co-ordination equilibrium X has feature f. (iii) If the fact that X is f is to lead to unambiguous results, then it must be mutually believed* that X is the only co-ordination equilibrium which is mutually believed* to be conspicuously f.

But these three conditions are far from being sufficient, for they will be met by all co-ordination equilibria in all co-ordination problems. For example, it will be mutual knowledge* amongst the parachutists that one building is in the upper left of the map area, another is in the upper right, and a third in the lower right. In some sense, however, these features of the possible meeting places balance each other off: there is no more reason why one should expect the other to go to the only building in the upper left area than there is for expecting him to go to the only building in the upper right area. It might, then, be made a fourth condition that it should not be mutually believed* by the agents involved that there is some analogous feature *g* which uniquely applies to an alternative co-ordination equilibrium. But this is vague and to some extent question-begging, even though its intended application may be clear. At any rate, it may stay for the moment, for it is still possible for two co-ordination equilibria to meet each of conditions (i)–(iv) and for one of them to have a certain feature which will unambiguously lead to the mutual expectation* that that co-ordination equilibrium will be the one adopted. For example, let us change our description of the parachutists' problem by supposing that it is mutual knowledge* between the two parachutists that two previous parachutists were in the same predicament and that they succeeded in meeting by going to the building represented in the upper left corner of the map. In this event, the present two parachutists will almost certainly expect one another to go to the building represented in the upper left corner of the map. For in this case it will be mutual knowledge* between them that a certain co-ordination equilibrium—their both going to a certain building—has the feature of being that co-ordination equilibrium adopted by two previous parachutists in the same predicament. This feature is one which they mutually know* to relate that co-ordination equilibrium more specifically or directly to their present co-ordination problem than does any other feature of any other co-ordination equilibrium, and therefore they will be provided with an unequivocal basis for expecting one another to go to the building represented in the upper left of the map.

So we might say, again somewhat metaphorically, that if the agents involved in a certain co-ordination problem *P* mutually know* (believe*) that each is aware that a certain co-ordination equilibrium *X* has a certain feature(s) *f* which relates *X* more specifically to *P* than does any other feature of any other co-ordination equilibrium, then, on the basis of this fact, it will be mutually known* (believed*) by them that each expects the others to act in accordance with co-ordination equilibrium *X*.

It is important to note that the case in which the relevant expectations are formed on the basis of an agreement between the agents is not an alternative to the case in which the relevant expectations are formed on the basis of its being mutual knowledge* that a certain co-ordination equilibrium has a certain unique and conspicuous feature: if the agents agree to conform to a certain co-ordination equilibrium X, then they will expect one another to conform to X because X has the feature of being that co-ordination equilibrium which they agreed to conform to.

V.3. *Convention*

On the basis of the above account of co-ordination problems it is not difficult to see how a convention might arise and perpetuate itself amongst a group of people for whom a certain type of co-ordination problem is recurrent.

Suppose that a certain type of co-ordination problem is recurrent in a group G. The problem may be of such a nature that each time it arises those involved may discuss beforehand which co-ordination equilibrium they will adopt: sometimes they will adopt one co-ordination equilibrium, sometimes they will adopt another. For example, the problem may be one of who should wash and who should dry the dishes, and here there may be no utility to having a convention. But the problem may be of such a nature as not conveniently to allow for discussion each time it arises; for instance, the problem may be one of deciding which side of the road one is to drive on. If an initial agreement is possible, members of G likely to be involved in the ordination problem may agree in advance always to conform to a certain co-ordination equilibrium whenever that co-ordination problem arises. This will secure its being mutual knowledge* amongst the members of G that a certain co-ordination equilibrium has the feature of being that co-ordination equilibrium members of G have agreed to conform to whenever they are agents in that co-ordination problem; and this will secure its being mutual knowledge* in G that members of G expect one another to conform to that co-ordination equilibrium whenever they are agents in that co-ordination problem; and this, in turn, will result in members of G conforming to that co-ordination equilibrium whenever they are involved in that co-ordination problem. And this, in turn, will result in their continuing to expect one another to conform to that co-ordination equilibrium when involved in that co-ordination problem, which will result in their continuing to conform to that co-ordination equilibrium when involved in that co-ordination problem, which will result in their continuing to expect one another to conform to that co-ordination equilibrium, which will result in their continuing to conform to that co-ordination equilibrium. This will result in that co-ordination equilibrium coming to have the feature of being that co-ordination equilibrium which members of G have always conformed to when they have been involved in that co-ordination problem, so that even when the original agreement has been forgotten, the fact that this practice is entrenched will result in their continuing to expect one another to conform to that co-ordination equilibrium, which will result in their continued conformity, which will result in the continued expectation of conformity, which will result in the continued conformity, and so on and on. It does not matter how such a practice becomes entrenched, but when a regularity becomes self-perpetuating in this way, it is a convention. Thus, in the United Kingdom there is a convention to drive on the left. Driving on public highways is a co-ordination problem and everyone's driving on the left is a co-ordination equilibrium in that co-ordination problem. The fact that it is mutual knowledge* amongst the drivers in the U.K. that there is this practice of driving on the left secures that everyone expects everyone to drive on the left, which secures that everyone will drive on the left, which secures that driving on the left will continue to be that co-ordination equilibrium which has the feature of being that to which everyone has conformed, which secures that everyone will continue to expect everyone to drive on the left, which secures that everyone will continue to drive on the left, and so on, at least until there is a change in the law which would eventually result in the entrenchment of a practice of driving on the right, in which case there will come to be a convention in the U.K. to drive on the right.

Let us begin with Lewis and say that:

there is a convention in G to do an act (of type) X in a (type of) situation C iff whenever any member of G is involved in (an instance of) C, he does X, and he does X because he expects the other members of G who are involved with him in C to do X, and he prefers to do X if they do since C is a coordination problem and doing X is a coordination equilibrium in C.[11]

(I have changed Lewis's wording somewhat, but this is the rough account of convention he offers before he "hides the concept beneath its refinements". It is important to note that substituends for 'X' may be logically complex; e.g., a convention to "call back if one is the original caller . . .".)

[11] *Convention*, p. 42.

This definition will have to be amended in at least two respects before it will yield a set of jointly sufficient conditions. First, it needs to be specified that it is mutual knowledge* amongst the members of G that the conditions of the analysans obtain. I trust that the reasons for this addition are familiar enough by now.[12] A second revision which needs to be made (which was not made by Lewis) is that the mutual knowledge* that members of G will do X when in situation C is based on their mutual knowledge* that there is a precedent in G of doing (or an agreement in G to do) X in situations of type C. The reasons for this are essentially the same as those offered in section V.1. It is, however, worth noticing that just as x might (nc) mean "p" in G even though no member of G has ever uttered x, so there may be a convention in G to do X in situations of type C even though no member of G has ever done X. Thus, there may be conventions governing behaviour in case of enemy attack which have never been acted upon because there has never been an enemy attack. In such a case we want to secure that members of G do not expect one another to conform to a certain co-ordination equilibrium as a result of that co-ordination equilibrium having a certain "natural" feature which renders it conspicuously unique; for if this were the case, then the knowledge that members of G will do X when in situations of type C would not be knowledge of a convention.

Once these two amendments are made, we will have a set of conditions jointly sufficient for the existence of a convention. But not all of the conditions will be separately necessary.

A convention, according to the above analysis, is a regularity in the behaviour of members of a group which constitutes a solution to a recurring co-ordination problem. But (1) for there to be a convention in G to do X in a type of situation C it is not necessary that doing X be a solution to a *recurring* co-ordination problem (i.e., C need not be a co-ordination problem), and (2) it is not necessary that doing X be in any sense a solution to any co-ordination problem (it is here that I part company with Lewis).

(1) Some conventions constitute solutions not to a recurring co-ordination problem, but to a single co-ordination problem that lasts over a long stretch of time. In a case of this type the agents involved have some common end which can be achieved only if they

---

[12] Lewis, faced with counter-examples similar to those discussed in section II.1, has defined a concept of "common knowledge" which in its essentials is the same as my "mutual knowledge*". The two accounts were arrived at independently.

regularly co-ordinate their actions in certain ways over time. For example, the workers on a farm may divide up the land between them so that each person farms a certain part of the land each day. That each person farms the land he does constitutes a convention. In this case the end to be brought about by co-ordination is a harvest of all the land, but that is something which happens only once every year.

(2) Most important, co-ordination problems, recurrent or otherwise, are not necessary for the existence of conventions. Conventions of meaning provide the best examples of conventions that are not solutions to co-ordination problems. If there prevails in G a convention to do X in a situation C and if C is a co-ordination problem and doing X is part of a co-ordination equilibrium, then when a member of G does X when in a situation C, he does X because he is expected to do X, and by doing what he is expected to do he thereby manages to co-ordinate his action with the actions of the other agents involved, thereby securing some common end. If, on the other hand, we have a convention to utter x only when one means thereby that p, then members of G will expect one another to utter x only if one means thereby that p; therefore, when a member of G utters x, he does so because it is believed (expected) that if one utters x, one will mean thereby that p. But here one does what, as it were, one is expected to do to secure that a certain inference is made, not to secure that one co-ordinates one's action with the actions of certain other agents. What is common to a convention to drive on the left and a convention to utter x only when one means thereby that p is that in both cases one does what the convention prescribes because everyone expects everyone to do so, but the cases differ relevantly in the way that others' expectations serve as a reason for doing what one does : in the former case one does what others expect one to do in order to co-ordinate one's action with the actions of certain others, whereas in the latter case one does what is expected in order to secure that a certain inference is made in the surest possible way.

It might appear that we could regard meaning conventions as solutions to co-ordination problems over time : in uttering x to mean thereby that p, S seeks to co-ordinate his action with the actions of other speakers (including himself) at other times; the common goal achieved by such co-ordination is facility of communication. But this suggestion involves a falsification of the

L

facts. *S*'s intention in uttering *x* is not to co-ordinate his action with that of other speakers in *G* so that he will thereby contribute to the facility of communication in *G*. He utters *x* in order to communicate to *A* that *p*, and he is able to do so as a result of there being a convention in *G* to utter *x* only when one means thereby that *p*. Besides, if such conventions are conceived of as solutions to co-ordination problems over time, then so must *all* conventions: in driving on the left in the U.K. I am not only co-ordinating my driving with the other drivers driving on the same road at the same time, I am also co-ordinating my driving with all drivers at all times and on all roads in the U.K., thereby contributing to the facility of road travel in the U.K.

In addition to conventions of meaning, most of the conventions of etiquette do not seem to involve co-ordination problems. For example, in most European countries there is a convention to hold the fork in the left hand, whereas in the U.S. the convention is to hold the fork in the right hand while eating from the fork. In some places, or amongst certain types of people, there prevails a convention for men to open doors for women. Conventions such as these are like the conventions considered above in that there is a precedent, or set of precedents, in a certain group for doing a certain sort of act (or activity) *X* in certain sorts of circumstances *C*; on the basis of this precedent everyone expects everyone else to do *X* when in circumstances *C*, everyone expects everyone to expect everyone to do *X* in *C*, etc.; and because it is expected, people do *X* when in circumstances *C*. What is not so immediately clear in the two preceding examples is why one should do what one is expected to do. Perha⊃s women expect men to open doors for them because it is the precedented thing to do; men continue to open doors for women because they do not want to upset women by acting contrary to their expectations; and the fact that men continue to open doors for women secures that women will continue to expect men to open doors for women, which secures that men will continue to open doors for women . . .

A more difficult case to decide is a convention to accept tokens of type *x* in exchange for goods and services of a certain value. I accept *x* for goods of a certain value because I expect others in turn to accept *x* from me in exchange for goods or services of that value, and I have this expectation because I expect everyone else to expect everyone else to accept tokens of type *x* in exchange for goods and services of that value. Thus, tokens of type x, things which are in themselves intrinsically worthless, have a certain value for the members of a certain group because it is mutual knowledge* amongst the members of that group that any member of the group engaged in trade will accept tokens of type x in exchange for goods and services of a certain value. To the extent that what one accepts in exchange for certain goods is dependent upon what one expects others to accept in exchange for goods of comparable value, situations of exchange resemble standard co-ordination problems. But there are also significant disanalogies. In the paradigm co-ordination problem there are two or more people each, as it were, trying to figure out what certain others expect him to do so that he may act in conformity with their expectations, thereby combining his actions with their combined actions in such a way as to bring about a certain result each desires. In a situation of exchange, however, there is no specific result several agents seek to secure by means of co-ordination, and the type of co-ordination that is found lacks the kind of symmetry found in the standard co-ordination problem; for example, when I accept x for y I may try to co-ordinate my action with the actions of certain other people in the future, but they do not seek to co-ordinate their acceptance of x with my acceptance of x.

What do these conventions have in common, whether or not they involve solutions to co-ordination problems?

In each case there is some (type of) action or activity X (e.g., driving on the left; uttering 'grrr'; giving pieces of green paper of a certain sort) which every member of G expects every other member of G to perform when (or only when) conditions of a certain sort obtain (e.g., driving on a public highway; communicating that one is angry; making a certain sort of exchange). The fact that everyone expects everyone to do X when (or only when) ... is a reason for anyone's doing X when (or only when). . . But— and here is what distinguishes the different types of convention— the reason why others' expectations are a reason for doing X is not the same in all cases: in some cases (e.g., driving on the left) one does what one is expected to do in order to co-ordinate one's action with the actions of certain others, thereby securing that some mutually desired end (e.g., the avoidance of collision) is achieved; in the case of a convention to utter x only when one means thereby that p, one does what one is expected to do in order to secure that a certain inference is made in the surest way possible; and so on. Finally, in each type of convention it is mutual knowledge* in G that there is a precedent (agreement) in G for doing X when (or only when) . . ., and it is on the basis of this that it is mutual knowledge* in G that members of G expect one another to do X, and so will do X, when (or only when) . . .

So I submit the following account of convention as being at least approximately correct.

> There prevails in G a convention to do an act (or activity) of type X when (or only when) . . . iff it is mutual knowledge* amongst the members of G that
>
> (1) there is a precedent in G for doing X, or an agreement or stipulation that one will do X, when (or only when) . . .;
> (2) on the basis (in part) of (1), almost everyone in G expects almost everyone in G to do X when (or only when) . . .;
> (3) because of (2), almost everyone in G does X when (or only when) . . .

If there is a convention in G to utter x only when (or when) one means thereby that p, then x will (*nc*) mean "p" in G; but there being such a convention is not, as noted in section V.1, a necessary condition of x (*nc*) meaning "p" in G. Yet I also concurred with the platitude that meaning is a matter of convention. There is, however, nothing paradoxical about this: an account of what it is for there to be a convention does not exhaust all of the relevant senses of 'convention'. x might (*nc*) mean "p" in G even though there is in G no convention to utter x when (or only when) . . .; but if x (*nc*) means "p" in G, then x will be a *conventional means* for meaning that p. Analogously, x may be a conventional means (medium) of exchange in G even though there is in G no convention to trade by exchanging tokens of type x.

Conventions result from the fact that there are certain ends which can be brought about by doing an act of a certain sort if and only if there is mutual knowledge* of a certain sort between certain people. But the kind of knowledge required is not the same for every type of convention. For example, in cases involving a co-ordination problem it is crucial that it be mutual knowledge* that anyone in a certain sort of situation will do X (e.g., that people will drive on the left). In other cases, however, what it is crucial to know is *not* that one *will* do X in a certain sort of situation, but only that *if* one does X, then such-and-such will be the case. Thus, for communication to be possible it is not necessary that it be known what people will utter; what is essential is that it be known that if someone utters x (in such-and-such circumstances), then he will mean such-and-such. Similarly, for trade to be successful it is not essential that we know what will be offered in exchange for goods and services, but only that if one accepts x in exchange for goods of a certain value, then one will be able to exchange x with someone else for goods of comparable value. It is this distinction which allows for the possibility of x being a conventional means for communicating that p (or a conventional means of exchange) without there being a convention to utter x only when (or when) one means that p (or a convention to trade by exchanging tokens of type x).

VI

UTTERANCE-MEANING AND LANGUAGE

VI.1 *Whole-utterance types*

If x (*nc*) means "*p*", then one knows what would be meant by uttering x on the basis of knowing what has been meant by uttering x. If, on the other hand, x is a composite whole-utterance type, one is able to know what someone meant by uttering x even though x is a novel utterance, that is, an utterance never before uttered. It is because composite whole-utterance types are constructions out of antecedently familiar items that one is able to know what would be meant by uttering a given composite whole-utterance type. If x is a composite whole-utterance type, one knows what would be meant by uttering x on the basis of one's knowledge of certain conventions or precedents pertaining to the constituents of x. Accordingly, the following account of what it is for a whole-utterance type x to mean "*p*" in a group G (for short, '$x(w)$ means "*p*" in G'), regardless of whether x is a composite or non-composite whole-utterance type, should cover all or most central and non-peripheral cases.

> $x(w)$ means "*p*" in G iff there prevails in G a convention or set of conventions Z such that any member of G acts in accordance with Z only if he utters x *M*-intending to produce in some other member of G the activated belief that p.

This account will do for our subsequent purposes, but for a completely general account I offer the following.

> $x(w)$ means "*p*" in G iff it is mutual knowledge* amongst the members of G that

> (1) if almost any member of G utters something *M*-intending to produce in some other member of G the activated belief that p, then what he utters might be x;

(2) if any member of G utters x M-intending to produce in some other member of G the activated belief that p, he will intend the state of affairs E (which he intends to realize by uttering x) to include the fact that there obtains in G a certain precedent or set of precedents (or agreements) Z such that any member of G utters x in accordance with Z only if he utters x M-intending to produce in some other member of G the activated belief that p.

Similar accounts may be given of what it is for x to (w) mean "so-and-so is to ψ" in G.

If it were not for a qualification to be made later, it would, I think, be misleading but not incorrect to say that x(w) means something in G just in case, for some p and some ψ, x (w) means "p" in G or x(w) means "so-and-so is to ψ" in G; in other words, x(w) means something in G just in case, for some p and some ψ, x is in G a conventional means for meaning that p or a conventional means for meaning that so-and-so is to ψ. This is correct because it provides a necessary and sufficient condition for x(w) meaning something in G. It is misleading because it fails to reflect the fact that specifications of what x(w) means may be of forms other than "p" or "so-and-so is to ψ". For example, the proposed necessary and sufficient condition for x(w) meaning something in G provides no way of reflecting the difference in meaning between 'What time is it?' and 'Inform me of the time!'. For each of these sentences is a conventional means for meaning that so-and-so is to inform one of the time, but they are not equivalent in meaning. To know the meaning of 'Inform me of the time!' is just to know that it is a conventional means for meaning that so-and-so is to inform one of the time, but to know the meaning of 'What time is it?' is to know that it is a conventional means for *requesting* so-and-so to inform one of the time.

So we want an account of what it is for x to (w) mean something that will enable us to specify fully what x(w) means. To get such an account it will be helpful to introduce some notation.

Let us say that x(w) means something in G just in case there is a proposition p such that x is in G either a conventional means for getting one's audience actively to believe that p (etc.) or a conventional means for getting one's audience to make it the case that p (etc.). (I am still ignoring a qualification to be made

below.) To say that there is a proposition p such that one utters
x intending A to make it the case that p (etc.) is equivalent to
saying that there is a type of act ψ such that one utters x intending
to get A to ψ (etc.).

I will now say that, for any p, $x(w)$ means "⊢$[p]$" in G just in
case x is in G a conventional means for meaning that p; and I
will say that, for any p, $x(w)$ means "!$[p]$" in G just in case x is
in G a conventional means for meaning that so-and-so is to make
it the case that p. If $x(w)$ means something in G, then, for some p,
x *must* (w) mean in G *at least* "⊢$[p]$" or "!$[p]$" and x *may* (w) mean
at most "⊢$[p]$" or "!$[p]$".

Commonly, as remarked in Chapter IV, when S means that p,
there is some truth-supporting reason (or reasons) ρ such that S
intends it to be mutual knowledge* between S and his audience
A that S intends A to have ρ as his reason, or part of his reason,
for believing that p; and commonly when S means that a certain
audience A is to make it the case that p, there is a reason (or
reasons) ρ such that S intends it to be mutual knowledge*
between S and A that S intends A to have ρ as his reason, or part
of his reason, for making it the case that p. So there clearly may
be a point to having a whole-utterance type x which is a conventional means not merely for making known that, say, S
uttered x intending to get A to make it the case that p, but also
a conventional means for making known that S intends A to
have a certain reason (or reasons) ρ for making it the case that p.
(Compare and contrast the difference in conventional force
between the sentences 'Inform me of the time!' and 'What time
is it?')

Let us introduce the additional notations '⊢$/\rho(t)$ $[p]$' and
'!$/\rho$ $[p]$'. We may now say that, for any p and any ρ, $x(w)$ means
"⊢$/\rho(t)[p]$" in G just in case x is in G a conventional means for
activating in one's audience the belief that $p/\rho(t)$ (etc.); and we
may say that, for any p and any ρ, $x(w)$ means "!$/\rho[p]$" in G just
in case x is in G a conventional means for getting one's audience
to make it the case that p/ρ (etc.).

Finally, I submit that, subject to a certain qualification,

$x(w)$ means something in G iff, for some p and some ρ, $x(w)$
means in G "⊢$[p]$" or "⊢$/\rho(t)$ $[p]$" or "!$[p]$" or "!$/\rho$ $[p]$".

$x(w)$ means something iff there is a group G such that $x(w)$
means something in G.

$x(w)$ means "⊢$[p]$" (or "⊢$/\rho(t)$ $[p]$" or . . .) iff there is a group G such that $x(w)$ means in G "⊢$[p]$" (or "⊢$/\rho(t)$ $[p]$" or . . .).

I further submit that

> x is a whole-utterance token which means ". . ." iff someone meant ". . ." by x.

To specify the meaning of an utterance x is to provide a completion for

> x means ". . ."

such that the expression replacing '. . .' has the same meaning as x (or has the same meaning as one of the meanings of x). Consequently, we may provide the following rule: if x means "⊢$[p]$" (or "⊢$/\rho(t)$ $[p]$" or . . .), then '⊢$[p]$' (or '⊢$/\rho(t)$ $[p]$' or . . .) may be replaced *salva veritate* by a sentence σ just in case σ means "⊢$[p]$" (or "⊢$/\rho(t)$ $[p]$" or . . .).

Now for the qualification referred to above. Our account of what it is for x to (w) mean something needs to be revised, for, contrary to what I have been pretending, it is not a necessary condition for $x(w)$ meaning something that there be a proposition p such that x is a conventional means either for activating in one's audience the belief that p (etc.) or for getting one's audience to make it the case that p (etc.). Consider, for instance, the sentence 'It is green.' or a non-composite whole-utterance type which means "it is green". There is no proposition p such that either of these utterance-types is a conventional means for activating in one's audience the belief that p (etc.). However, if S subscriptively utters 'It is green.' then there is (thought by S to be) an item y such that S intends his utterance of 'It is green.' to activate in some A the belief that y is green (likewise if S subscriptively utters a non-composite whole-utterance type which means "it is green"). Perhaps the following will provide an approximate set of necessary and sufficient conditions for $x(w)$ meaning something in G.

> $x(w)$ means something in G iff there is a convention or set of conventions Z and a set of functions F such that it is mutual knowledge* amongst the members of G that Z prevails in G and either (1) any member of G, S, utters x in accordance with Z only if for some function f which belongs to F there

is a sequence of items i (or so S believes) and a proposition p such that S intends his audience to recognize that $f(x,i) = p$, and S means that p by uttering x, or (2) any member of G, S, utters x in accordance with Z only if for some function f' which belongs to F there is a sequence of items i (or so S believes) and a proposition p such that S intends his audience A to recognize that $f'(x, i) = p$, and S means by uttering x that A is to make it the case that p.[1]

(Notice that this definition relies on the assumption that there are sets of functions which map sentence tokens and sequences of items onto propositions.)

I shall leave for some other occasion the difficult task of providing a more comprehensive scheme to replace that given on pages 157 and 158.

VI.2 *Language*

If x is a composite whole-utterance type which means "⊢$[p]$" in G, then there will prevail in G a set of conventions Z such that one utters x in accordance with Z only if one means by uttering x that p. But what sort of conventions must prevail in G if members of G are to communicate with one another by producing composite and perhaps novel whole-utterance types? Moreover, what sort of conventions must prevail in G if it is to be true of members of G that they have a language? To rule out the very least interesting cases we may agree that acceptance of a system of conventions Z will not constitute having a language unless Z has what we might call the two features of *compositeness* and *recursiveness*. Z has the feature of *compositeness* just in case the whole-utterance types generated by Z are composite; that is, on the basis of their knowledge of a finite set of conventions pertaining to a finite set of items, members of G are able to communicate with one another by producing novel combinations of those items. Z has the feature of *recursiveness* just in case there are an infinite number of whole-utterance types generated by Z; that is, on the basis of their knowledge of a finite set of conventions pertaining to a finite set of items, members of G are in principle able to produce and understand an infinite number of whole-utterance types. As will soon be apparent, these two requirements are indeed minimal requirements.

[1] I am primarily indebted to Brian Loar for the form of this definition, but George Myro improved on an earlier version.

A theory of meaning for a particular language L is a finite set of conditions from which follows for each of the infinite number of sentences of L a true statement of the form: *sentence σ means* . . . The question now to be asked—one which subsumes the two preceding questions—is: What general form must an adequate theory of meaning for a particular language take?[2]

Let us approach an answer to this question in three stages. In the first stage I will informally characterize a very simple language L, but one which has the two features of compositeness and recursiveness. In the second stage I will attempt to provide a theory of meaning for L; and in the third stage a general answer will be offered to the general question about the form of a theory of meaning for any language.

Language L has three proper names, 'a', 'b', and 'c', which respectively designate the objects A, B, and C, three predicates, 'F', 'G' and 'H', which respectively express the properties *red*, *green*, and *blue*, and two truth-functional constants, '—' and '&', which are respectively equivalent to the English words 'not' and 'and'. Let us call the marks 'a', 'b', and 'c' the N's, and the marks 'F', 'G', and 'H' the V's. A string (of marks) σ is a sentence of L just in case it satisfies one of the following conditions. (1) σ has the form VN; (2) there is a sentence ϕ such that σ consists of '—', followed by ϕ; (3) there are sentences ϕ and ψ such that σ consists of ϕ, followed by '&', followed by ψ.

Thus, 'Fa', '$Fa \& Gb$' and '$—Hc$' are sentences of L. 'Fa' means "A is red"; '$Fa \& Gb$' means "A is red and B is green"; and '$—Hc$' means "C is not blue".

Now the problem is to provide a theory of meaning for L, one which makes no use of any semantical notion other than S-meaning.

Consider a rather simple and direct approach to this problem. Would we not have an adequate theory of meaning for L, at least with regard to the atomic sentences of L, if the following conventions prevailed amongst the speakers of L?

(I) If anyone utters 'a' preceded by a V, he means thereby that A has the property correlated by the relevant convention with that V.

Similarly for the other N's.

---

[2] I am indebted to Brian Loar for the idea of putting the matter in this way. I am also indebted to him for nearly every other idea contained in this section.

(II) If anyone utters 'F' followed by an N, he means thereby that the object correlated by the relevant convention with that N is red.

Similarly for the other V's.

To this simple and direct approach there is a conclusive and obvious objection, one which I had not noticed until it was pointed out by Brian Loar. Consider the sentence 'Fa'. Our theory of meaning for L will be adequate only if it follows from the proposed conventions that 'Fa' means "A is red". But it follows from convention (II) that anyone uttering 'Fa' will mean that the object correlated by convention with 'a' is red, and, *a fortiori*, it follows that 'Fa' will mean "the object correlated by convention with 'a' is red". But 'the object correlated by convention with 'a' is red' does not mean the same as 'A is red', so we have failed to capture the meaning of 'Fa'. (The same point follows, *mutatis mutandis*, with respect to convention (I) and with respect to conventions (I) and (II) taken conjointly.) The difficulty, of course, is that the context 'x means . . .' is intensional, and so we cannot substitute in it, *salva veritate*, expressions which are not logically equivalent.

Loar has suggested a more sophisticated approach, one which makes use of the Tarskian conception of a semantic definition of truth and adds an intensional element to it.[3]

We define a condition on the strings of marks which were specified syntactically above; call it condition C. As a preliminary to its definition:

(1) Let M be the set of ordered pairs: $\{\langle 'a', A\rangle, \langle 'b', B\rangle, \langle 'c', C\rangle\}$.

(2) Let M' be the set of ordered pairs: $\{\langle 'F', \text{redness}\rangle, \langle 'G', \text{greenness}\rangle, \langle 'H', \text{blueness}\rangle\}$.

Range of variables: 'V' ranges over the V's, 'N' over the N's, 'y' over objects, and 'P' over properties of objects.

(3) (*Condition C*) A string σ satisfies condition C iff there is a V, an N, a y, and a P such that:

(a_1) σ consists of V, followed by N; and

(a_2) $\langle N, y\rangle$ is a member of M; and

(a_3) $\langle V, P\rangle$ is a member of M'; and

(a_4) y has P; or

---

[3] In some unpublished papers and in conversation.

(b) there is a sentence ϕ such that σ consists of '—', followed by ϕ, and ϕ does not satisfy condition C;[4] or

(c) there are sentences ϕ and ψ such that σ consists of ϕ, followed by '&', followed by ψ, and ϕ and ψ satisfy condition C.

Condition C is so defined that any sentence of L is true just in case it satisfies C; but it does not follow from the fact that a certain string of marks satisfies C that that string has any semantical properties whatever. What more is needed, then, in order for us to have an adequate theory of meaning for L? On the assumption that L is the language of group G, it may seem that our theory of meaning for L will be complete if

there prevails in G a convention to refrain from uttering any sentence of L, σ, unless there is a proposition p such that σ meets C iff p and one means by uttering σ that p.

I have suggested that $x(w)$ means "$\vdash[p]$" in G if there prevails in G a convention or set of conventions Z such that one utters x in accordance with Z only if one means that p by uttering x. Now 'Fa' meets condition C just in case A is red. So, it may seem, there prevails in G a convention such that one utters 'Fa' in accordance with that convention only if one means by uttering 'Fa' that A is red. It should therefore follow, as desired, that 'Fa' means "A is red" in G. But this argument is invalid. For suppose that there is a proposition—say, the proposition that grass is green—which has the same truth-value as the proposition that A is red. In that event, 'Fa' will meet condition C if and only if grass is green; and so it will be possible for one to utter 'Fa' in accordance with the above convention and mean thereby that grass is green. In other words, one could utter 'Fa' in accordance with the convention and not mean that A is red.

Notice, however, that in order to utter 'Fa' in accordance with the convention and mean thereby that grass is green one has to know certain facts about the world in addition to knowing what must be the case if 'Fa' is to satisfy condition C: one must know that the proposition that A is red and the proposition that grass is green have the same truth-value. Consequently, the problem

---

[4] A string σ is a sentence, as that word is here used, just in case it meets the conditions for a string being a sentence given in the informal characterization of L. Thus, no questions are begged concerning the semantical properties of such strings.

before us would not arise if members of G meant that p by uttering σ only if their knowledge that σ satisfies C if and only if p were based solely on their knowledge of what must be the case if σ is to satisfy C. Here, then, we have a new twist to the old distinction between knowledge of language or meaning, and knowledge of fact.

Loar has suggested the following detailed revision to secure an adequate theory of meaning for L.

First, let $R =$ some minimum degree of rationality; in particular, that degree of rationality possessed by any speaker of any language.

Next, let us say that

for any sentence of L, σ, and for any proposition p, σ *C-determines* p iff

(1) σ meets C iff p;
(2) if anyone both possesses R and believes that σ meets C, he believes that p, where p is some proposition other than that σ meets C.

Finally, we may restate the above convention thus:

there prevails in G a convention to refrain from uttering any sentence of L, σ, unless there is a proposition p such that σ *C*-determines p and one means by uttering σ that p.

From this it should follow that each of the infinite number of sentences of L has that meaning assigned to it in our informal characterization of L.

Imagine now a slightly more complicated language L', which contains L along with an imperative mood. In L' there is the sign '!', and if σ is a sentence of L, then σ preceded by '!' is a sentence of L', and if σ means "⊢$[p]$" in L, then σ preceded by '!' means "!$[p]$" in L'. (Thus, 'Fa' and '!Fa' are sentences of L'; 'Fa' means "A is red" and '!Fa' means "so-and-so is to make it the case that A is red".) To introduce imperatives in L, thereby giving us L', we need only add that there prevails in G a convention to refrain from uttering any sentence of L, σ preceded by '!', unless there is a proposition p such that σ *C*-determines p and, for some A, one means by uttering σ preceded by '!' that A is to make it the case that p.

It would be highly rewarding to continue complicating L until we had a language with quantifiers, indicator words, modal operators, etc.; that is, until we had a language resembling a full-blown natural language. This is a task I gladly leave to others more qualified than I.

Still, we can generalize from our simple example and offer what is at least a first approximation to an answer on the lines suggested by Loar to the question "What general form must an adequate theory of meaning for a particular language take?" If the members of a group G have a language, then there is a syntactical feature g, a syntactical feature g', a set of conditions C, and a set of conventions Z such that for any string σ, S utters σ in accordance with Z only if there is a sequence of items i (or so S believes) such that S intends A to recognize that σ and i C-determine p, and if σ has g, then S means that p, and if σ has g', then S means that A is to make it the case that p. (Thus, C-determination applies not only to indicative sentences, and the satisfaction or non-satisfaction of C is a broader matter than truth or non-truth.) We provide the theory of meaning for the language of G by specifying the values of 'g', 'g'', 'C' and 'Z', though, of course, specification of the value of 'Z' carries with it specification of the value of 'C'. (The reason for saying that σ and a sequence of items i C-determine p is this. In a sentence containing indicator words, such as 'She is kissing him', there will be no unique proposition which that sentence uniformly expresses. Rather, what proposition such a sentence expresses on a given occasion of its use will be a function of both the referred to items in a specific order [i.e., the relevant sequence of such items] and the sentence. For example, on the occasion of a particular utterance of 'She is kissing him' to mean that Jill is kissing Jack at t [where $t =$ the time of the utterance], S means what he does by virtue of there being a certain function f which maps the sequence of items Jill, Jack, and t and the sentence 'She is kissing him' onto the proposition that Jill is kissing Jack at t, where f is determined by the conventions of English in the way made clear by our analysis of a theory of meaning for a language. In the case of sentences not containing indicator words, $i =$ the null sequence; this is just a manner of speaking to enable us to achieve simplicity of exposition, for in such a case we could say that σ directly C-determines p.)

In section I.1, I said that in order to have a complete answer to the question "What is meaning?" we must provide an account of what it is for something to be a part-utterance type and of what it is for something to be a part-utterance type which means "...". I suggest that to know the meaning of a word is just to know what contributions it makes to the *C*-determination (for the relevant condition *C*) of the sentences in which it occurs. Beyond this suggestion I will not now venture, partly because I doubt that a single and univocal account can be given which would accommodate all of the different kinds of words there are. So I have not completely answered the question "What is meaning?": and even if I had we would still lack a complete theory of language and communication.

WORKS CITED

Alston, William P. *Philosophy of Language* (Prentice-Hall, Englewood Cliffs, New Jersey, 1964).

Austin, J. L. *How to Do Things with Words*, ed. J. O. Urmson (Oxford University Press, Oxford, 1962).

Cohen, L. J. "Do Illocutionary Forces Exist?", *Philosophical Quarterly*, 14 (1964), 118–37.

Grice, H. P. "Meaning", *Philosophical Review*, 66 (1957), 377–88.

—— "Utterer's Meaning and Intentions", *Philosophical Review*, 78 (1969), 147–77.

—— "Utterer's Meaning, Sentence-Meaning, and Word-Meaning", *Foundations of Language*, 4 (1968), 225–42.

Hume, David *A Treatise of Human Nature* (Ed. L. A. Selby-Bigge. Oxford: Clarendon Press, 1888).

Lewis, David K. *Convention: A Philosophical Study* (Harvard University Press, Cambridge, Mass., 1969).

Mates, Benson *Elementary Logic* (Oxford University Press, New York, 1965).

Rawls, John "Two Concepts of Rules", *Philosopical Review*, 64 (1955), 3–32.

Schelling, Thomas C. *The Strategy of Conflict* (Harvard University Press, Cambridge, Mass., 1960).

Searle, John R. "Austin on Locutionary and Illocutionary Acts", *Philosophical Review*, 77 (1968), 405–24.

—— *Speech Acts: An Essay in the Philosophy of Language* (Cambridge University Press, Cambridge, 1969).

—— "What is a Speech Act?", in Max Black (ed.), *Philosophy in America* (Allen & Unwin, London, 1965).

Strawson, P. F. "Intention and Convention in Speech Acts", *Philosophical Review*, 73 (1964), 439–60.

INDEX